WOODLAWN REMEMBERS

Cemetery of American History

by

Edward F. Bergman

with Preface by

Louis Auchincloss

Published by
North Country Books, Inc.
Utica, New York

WOODLAWN REMEMBERS
CEMETERY OF AMERICAN HISTORY

ISBN 0-932052-68-1

Library of Congress Cataloging-in-Publication Data

Bergman, Edward F.
    Woodlawn remembers: cemetery of American history/by Edward F.
Bergman.
       p.   cm.
    ISBN 0-932052-68-1 : $24.95
    1. Woodlawn Cemetery (New York, N.Y.) 2. New York (N.Y.)—
—Biography. 3. Celebrities—United States—Biography.
4. Sepulchral monuments—New York (N.Y.) I. Title.
F128.61.W8B46 1988
974.7'1—dc19   88-29105
                                                   CIP

published by
North Country Books, Inc.
Publisher — Distributor
18 Irving Place
Utica, New York 13501-5618

Dedication

*This book is dedicated to all those buried
at The Woodlawn Cemetery, famous or private.*

Acknowledgements

The author wishes to acknowledge the tremendous assistance of Mrs. Jeanne Capodilupo, Assistant to the President of The Woodlawn Cemetery; of all of the staff at Woodlawn from President Edward Laux to each and every groundskeeper; of photographer Dominick Totino; of Professor David Gillison; of many helpful librarians from New York to San Francisco, Minneapolis to Galveston; and, especially, of my family, for their generous support of this project.

Table of Contents

Preface

The democracy of death, so encompassing as almost to justify a platitude, makes us all equal, and celebrities in a graveyard, as the poets have always told us, are only mocked by the pretention of their monuments to stand out from the other ghosts. And yet the grim denominator of human extinction can give to a cemetery, especially in a rustic setting, a pathos that helps to redeem a pompous mausoleum and to enhance the charm of a lovely one. Woodlawn tells us an American story from so many different points of view that it would be meaningless were it not so dramatically united in a common fate. Belmonts and Baches share their resting place with actors and acrobats. Heroes of battle like Admiral Farragut are joined in the earth with heroes of scandal like Fatty Arbuckle. Edward Bergman has not tried to weave a coherence out of the sometimes beautiful, sometimes garish tombs or out of his brief lives of the multitudinous famed who inhabit them. He has let Woodlawn Cemetery speak for itself and give to the reader of his book whatever arcane message it has to convey.

Louis Auchincloss
President of the Museum of the City of New York

Woodlawn Remembers:
Cemetery of American History

Within Woodlawn Cemetery reposes the most remarkable variety of interesting and historically important people anywhere in America. Musician "Duke" Ellington, jurist Charles Evans Hughes, financier Jay Gould, author Herman Melville, journalist Nellie Bly, lawman Bat Masterson, inventor Gail Borden, and many more rest in this beautiful Arcadian setting. More fascinating people lie here than any of us could meet in a lifetime, and visiting Woodlawn and learning these peoples' stories can teach us a lot about our history and our national culture.

Americans experience change daily. We tear down and replace buildings almost overnight. We redesign and rebuild whole neighborhoods so frequently and rapidly that few places around us remain visual records of our past. Even our childhood homes may be gone. With Thomas Jefferson we say "putting up and pulling down is one of my favorite amusements." By doing this, however, we sacrifice a sense of continuity with our past. Our past remains for us to see in only a few places, such as our cemeteries. There we can learn about our forebearers, and about people we have honored in their own time.

AMERICANS' ATTITUDES TOWARD NATURE AND DEATH

A cemetery teaches us something about the deepest commitments and philosophies of the people who built it. This is especially true in America because our pastoral cemeteries reveal our attitude toward Nature. At the time of our national birth, European Romantics were just discovering the sublimity of Nature, but it is in America, the "New World," that we have felt a special affinity with it. We have always self-consciously contrasted the rawness of our original national landscape, the severity of our climate and the challenge of taming our wilderness with the over-cultivation of the Old World: its man-made prettiness, our natural grandeur. "Keep Britain tidy," they say. "Keep America beautiful," we reply.

1

This American Romantic-transcendentalism, part of our national cultural heritage, has also affected the way we view death. In 1811, seventeen-year-old William Cullen Bryant wrote what is still one of America's best-loved poems, "Thanatopsis." In this "Meditation on Death" Bryant advised:

> When thoughts
> Of the last bitter hour come like a blight
> Over thy spirit, and sad images. . . .
> Make thee to shudder, and grow sick at heart, —
> Go forth, under the open sky, and list
> To Nature's teachings. . . .
> . . . . Earth, that nourished thee, shall claim
> Thy growth, to be resolved to earth again. . . .
> So live, that when thy summons comes. . . .
> approach thy grave
> Like one who wraps the drapery of his couch
> About him, and lies down to pleasant dreams.

Death is a part of Nature, and our private consolation is to be found in reconciliation with Nature. To express this we have favored pastoral cemeteries designed not only as resting places for the dead, but also as places for the living to find solace and consolation in the contemplation of Nature. As the Scottish romantic Robert Louis Stevenson wrote, "There is a certain frame of mind to which a cemetery is, if not an antidote, at least an alleviation. If you are in a fit of the blues, go nowhere else." American cemeteries were actually our first open public places, precursors of our public parks.

CEMETERY DESIGN AND LOCATION

Cemeteries can vary in their design between two distinct models. One type, called a Necropolis, or "City of the Dead," is predominantly architectural. Monuments crowd upon one another and overwhelm Nature. This style can be traced back to Pisa's medieval Campo Santo, and it culminates in Genoa's Staglieno Cemetery (designed in 1844), which is a series of arcaded sculpture galleries. We do have a few of these cemeteries in America, such as Saint Louis Cemetery in New Orleans and Congressional Cemetery in Washington, D.C. Our general aversion to this type, however, was well expressed by Senator Hoar of Massachusetts when he saw the heavy cubic monuments Benjamin Latrobe designed for Congressional Cemetery. The thought of being buried beneath one of them, Hoar insisted, added new terror to death.

The contrasting model is the rural cemetery, which Americans generally prefer. It is pastoral, an Elysian Field, a garden of graves. While the word Necropolis means "City of the Dead," "cemetery" means "place of sleep." In a rural-style cemetery, Nature dominates. Picturesque monuments and memorials fit in as man fits into Nature, as death is a part of life.

Any individual cemetery reflects which of these two models was favored at the time of its creation. Through subsequent years changing tastes and, of course, the financial means of the people buried there record changes in social philosophies. We shall see this clearly at Woodlawn.

The question of designing cemeteries relates to the question of where they should be. The Ancient World buried its dead along roads leading out of the cities. Athens

Illustration One: The Cemetery of Père Lachaise opened outside Paris in 1804, taking its name from King Louis XIV's confessor, who had once owned the land. By the time of this print, about 1870, it had already lost its rural character, but Parisians nevertheless came to stroll among the monuments to loved ones or to admire monuments of the famous. (From a print in the author's collection.)

had its Dipylon Gate for this purpose, and Rome its Via Appia. Medieval Christianity brought burial into the city, in the churchyard or right into the church itself. But as cities expanded, small community cemeteries and churchyards ran out of room, and by 1800 most urbanites wanted new burial grounds established outside the city. This removal "back to Nature" conformed to the Romantic philosophy developing at the time.

WOODLAWN'S PRECEDENTS

Père Lachaise — Paris, France

The first rural cemetery designed as a retreat from the city was Père Lachaise, built outside Paris in 1804. The remains of great Frenchmen of the past were soon transferred to Père Lachaise with elaborate new monuments: the medieval lovers Abélard (1079-1142) and Héloise (1101-1164); France's greatest comic dramatist Molière (1622-1673); Jean de la Fontaine (1662-1695), poet and author of fables; and others. The cemetery's original purpose as an abode for the dead, to which had already been added the second function of a pastoral retreat for urban dwellers, slowly developed still a third function as a cultural institution. The cemetery became a place to view fine works of architecture and sculpture and also to foster patriotic and civic pride by honoring great individuals of the past. Just as families had traditionally tended family plots with loving respect and pride, so the new cemetery would emphasize the historical continuity of the nation.

The multiplication of monuments in Père Lachaise, however, quickly threatened the cemetery's original rural appearance (Illustration One). Art crowded out Nature. By 1825 over 26,000 monuments were recorded on Père Lachaise's 57 acres! Within ten years of its opening, guidebooks helped visitors find the graves of the famous and the most artistically significant monuments. Contemporaries were aware of the rapidly changing quality of the setting, and many criticized the loss of natural beauty from the cemetery. But Père Lachaise came to be more and more built up, and it was visited only as an art museum and gallery of great Frenchmen. Its original quality and its function as a pastoral retreat from the city were sacrificed.

Père Lachaise is still a major tourist attraction. It boasts two out of a possible three stars in the latest *Michelin Guide*, but the cemetery offers no communion with Nature.

Mount Auburn — Cambridge, Massachusetts

Mount Auburn Cemetery in Cambridge, Massachusetts, was America's first planned rural cemetery, nonsectarian and detached from any church. Boston physician and botanist, Doctor Jacob Bigelow, launched the campaign to build a new cemetery outside the city limits, and the Massachusetts Horticultural Society joined him because it wanted to build an "experimental garden." Leading scientific opinion held that cemetery air was unhealthy unless cleaned by circulation through trees, and so the Massachusetts Legislature authorized this cemetery-arboretum in 1831.

Mount Auburn Cemetery was immediately successful. It was preferred for interments, and its grounds offered an opportunity for strolling and meditating in a "rural" environment, providing welcome relief from urban congestion (Illustration Two). Proud Bostonians made a visit to Mount Auburn a "must" for visitors. Franklin Pierce was meditating under a tree at Mount Auburn when a boy brought him the news that he had received the Democratic Party presidential nomination in 1852. Mount Auburn even welcomed picnickers. The cemetery's site commands a beautiful view of the Charles River and of Boston.

Mount Auburn also served as an outdoor sculpture garden and as a classroom of national history, just as Père Lachaise did. When the great navigator Nathaniel Bowditch died in 1838, a committee of prominent citizens proposed to erect a memorial statue somewhere in the City of Boston. Within the five years it took to raise the money and to commission the statue from sculptor Ball Hughes, however, Mount Auburn itself, where Bowditch had been buried, had come to be felt as the most appropriate place for such monuments. Other leading American sculptors represented by works in Mount Auburn include Thomas Crawford, E. A. Brackett, Horatio Greenough and Henry Kirke.

Through the nineteenth century and into the early twentieth, cemeteries were assumed to be the appropriate site for the finest sculpture and stonecarving. Then the "modern" movement unfortunately repudiated this art form. An exhibition of American sculpture sponsored by New York's Museum of Modern Art in the 1930's specifi-

Illustration Two: Mount Auburn Cemetery in Cambridge, Massachusetts, was chartered in 1831 as America's first rural-style cemetery. This popular European print of 1839 shows a recognizable spot at Mount Auburn as something between the Garden of Eden and a jungle. Romantic landscape architects recommended the construction of lakes in which evening visitors could contemplate the reflected moon. (From a print in the author's collection.)

cally rejected cemetery work. Today, however, we again value this artistic richness. Nineteenth century stonecarvers are appreciated as fine artists, and earlier gravestones are studied carefully (Illustration Four).

Greenwood — Brooklyn, New York

Mount Auburn's success was soon followed by the planning of Greenwood Cemetery in Brooklyn, New York (Illustration Three). Brooklyn was, until 1898, a separate city from New York City, across the East River, and it grew rapidly in population and in wealth during the nineteenth century. In 1838 civic pride inspired a private group to commission prestigious surveyor and engineer David Bates Douglass to build a fine new "Necropolis" in suburban Brooklyn. The committee selected a commanding site with a beautiful harbor view, as at Mount Auburn, to please the living who were expected to visit. This was Douglass' first landscape commission, but he immediately rejected both the designated name and the Necropolis type of cemetery. He planned instead a rural-type cemetery to invite contemplation of Nature. Typical names for landscape features include Halcyon Lake, Vista Hill, Camelia Path and Sylvan Cliff. Because Romantic theory recommended that people

Illustration Three: Greenwood Cemetery, opened in Brooklyn in 1838, soon attracted thousands of visitors each year. A taste for Egyptian style funerary sculpture recurs periodically in America—between 1840 and 1860 was one cycle, and again in the 1920's. Superlative examples such as the Bache mausoleum can be seen at Woodlawn. (From an 1847 print in the author's collection.)

enjoy sheets of water reflecting moonlight, Douglass cut streams and dug six artificial lakes at Greenwood. The cemetery's scattered wooden shelters, all designed by the leading Romantic school architect, Richard Upjohn, exemplified various picturesque styles: Gothic Revival, Italian Villa and Swiss Chalet. The living were encouraged to visit—the main road winding through the property is "The Tour."

Greenwood soon became the region's leading tourist attraction. A popular description was printed in 1839, an illustrated guide in 1847, and the first directory to the graves of the famous in 1849. By mid-century some 60,000 people visited Greenwood each year; yes, even for strolls by moonlight.

Greenwood's administrators wanted to set a high standard for landscape design, and so, in 1875, they published a list of deciduous trees most appropriate for cemeteries.

CEMETERIES AND URBAN PUBLIC PARKS

The great popularity of rural-style cemeteries such as Mount Auburn and Greenwood demonstrated the need for public recreation space. Back in the nineteenth century recreation meant leisurely strolling and meditating, nothing so strenuous as ball games or jogging. And so the rural cemetery movement fathered the demand for urban public parks, which are a distinct American "invention." Poet William Cullen Bryant, in middle-age by mid-century, led the drive in New York City, which then had no rural cemetery. New York opened a design competition for a park in 1858, and when Calvert Vaux and Frederick Law Olmsted presented their winning plan for this, the world's first urban public park, it was no coincidence that the original name of their plan was "Greensward." Central Park, as it became, still offers a bit of pastoral calm in the middle of crowded Manhattan. Olmsted went on to design parks, college campuses and cemeteries across America.

Many years later, when Doctor Hubert Eaton built California's famous cemetery, Forest Lawn, he called it a "Memorial Park." "Forest Lawn," he said, "shall be not only a safe repository for our beloved dead, but a place for the sacred enjoyment of the living as well." "Memorial Park" was a new term, but the idea continued in the American cemetery tradition.

THE IMPETUS FOR WOODLAWN

The location of Woodlawn had brought it into historical prominence during the American Revolutionary War. In September 1776, George Washington evacuated New York City and retreated north into Westchester, where, in October, he made a stand at White Plains. In order to delay the pursuing British troops, Washington ordered General Heath to construct a redoubt at the southeast corner of what is today Woodlawn Cemetery. The redoubt's guns commanded the Bronx River Valley, the Boston Road and Williams' Bridge across the Bronx River. Today a plaque inside the Cemetery marks the site of that redoubt, and the principal street south of the Cemetery bridging the river is still called Gun Hill Road.

By the 1860's congestion on New York and Brooklyn city streets and on the ferries crossing the East River sabotaged the dignity of funeral processions from Manhattan out to Greenwood. There was no Brooklyn Bridge until 1883. Crowded streets and ferries "occasion delay," wrote *The New York Times*, "and often furnish sights and sounds very little in keeping with the wounded sensibilities of the sorrowing." Women were often actually prohibited from accompanying the remains of their loved ones out to the cemetery because of the indelicacy of the experiences along the way.

These circumstances led a group of New Yorkers to look around for a more accessible site to build a new cemetery. Following the route of the New York and Harlem Railroad to the North, they discovered the beautifully wooded Bronx River Valley, and there the Woodlawn Cemetery Association bought 313 acres in 1863. The land which the Association bought lay along the railroad line for about one-half mile just beyond Williams' Bridge across the Bronx River, and it extended westward to the summit of the crest between the Bronx River and the Hudson River watersheds. Williams' Bridge is only about ten miles north of 42nd Street in Manhattan, and special funeral trains from the city could reach the new Woodlawn station at the cemetery's northeast corner in thirty-five minutes. Special cars, one named "Woodlawn," were designed to transport the coffin and mourners. As late as 1903 the cost to rent a private funeral train to Woodlawn and back to Grand Central Station was still only fifty dollars.

Within a few years of Woodlawn's opening, a convenient wide avenue through the Bronx, which was not then a part of New York City, was constructed up to the cemetery's gate on its western side. This is Jerome Avenue, named for the capitalist Leonard Jerome, Winston Churchill's grandfather. He owned a nearby racetrack. Because Woodlawn Cemetery was now so easily accessible from New York City either by rail or carriage, its opening restored bereaved women to the funeral procession and to graveside ceremonies. Several members of the Jerome family rest in Woodlawn today, and the avenue is the route of New York City's No. 4 subway line, which terminates at Woodlawn.

While the new Woodlawn Cemetery was readily accessible from New York City, it was nevertheless "sufficiently remote from the island [of Manhattan] to be beyond the reach of its noise, and the apprehension and disturbance from the extension of the city limits," wrote the *Times* in 1866. "It is essentially a rural cemetery, and must remain so for generations to come." The *Times* was right that Woodlawn should retain its rural quality, but New York City and suburban growth long ago encroached upon its gates (Illustration Five). In fact, as some downtown churches have been demolished and old burying grounds built over, their dead have been reinterred at Woodlawn. Today Woodlawn contains not only numerous tombstones dating back into the eighteenth century, but even the remains of some of New York's earliest seventeenth century settlers.

WOODLAWN'S BEGINNINGS

Woodlawn's first modest interment was that of Mrs. Phoebe Underhill on January 14, 1865. The time, however, was a turning point in American history. Three months later Lee surrendered to Grant at Appomattox Courthouse, the Civil War ended, and the re-United States launched into a spectacular era of growth and wealth which we call the "Gilded Age." The City of New York and Woodlawn Cemetery would show this. New York City grew to dominate a burgeoning national economy, and the ambitious came from all over the country.

As the fabric of national life was rewoven, many Civil War heroes, both of the Union and of the Confederacy, would be buried in Woodlawn. Admiral David Farragut, who captured New Orleans in 1862, lies but a few hundred yards from Confederate General Mansfield Lovell (1822-1884), who defended that city. One son of New York's proud old Gracie family, whose ancestral mansion is today the mayor's official residence, married a Southerner and was directing a family-owned company in Alabama in 1861. Archibald Gracie III served as a general in the Confederate Army and was killed in action at Petersburg in 1864, at age thirty-two. His body was later returned to his native city for burial in the family plot. Still other Confederate generals and a surprising number of brothers who fought one another in the War lie side by side at Woodlawn.

Twentieth-century America was born with the construction of railroads and of steamships, the settlement of the West and the carving of new states, the expansion of industry and trade, the growing power of finance and of the press, the rise of the inventor-entrepreneur, and new cultural forms, including the multiplying contributions of black Americans and of women. America rose to become a world power. Dominant players in all these stories are buried at Woodlawn.

The stories told within these pages are not just the history of New York City, but of the United States. United States Senator William Clark built and represented Montana, and Senator Simon Guggenheim ruled Colorado. Gail Borden was a founding father of the Republic of Texas; his two sons fought on opposite sides in the Civil War. The Inman family was the "first family of Atlanta." William C. Durant's family

Illustration Four: **The Requiem** *says "A trumpet spreading a wondrous sound through the graves of all lands will drive mankind before the throne. Death and Nature shall be astonished when all creation rises again." This Woodlawn sculpture broods until she is bidden to raise her trumpet and sound that blast.*

pioneered in Michigan, and William's grandfather, who reared the boy, was the state's governor in the 1860's. William Ogden was "the man who built and owned Chicago"; he was that city's first mayor.

People buried at Woodlawn wrote much of the early history of San Francisco. In the 1850's William Webb's clipper ships set speed records connecting New York with that booming city, and Captain David Farragut built the United States Naval Station at Mare Island. Ferdinand Ewer was president of the San Francisco Board of Education and a leading journalist, while Lotta Crabtree performed just a few blocks away from where her later gift to San Francisco, Lotta's Fountain, still stands as an historic landmark. Collis P. Huntington visited San Francisco regularly in order to buy merchandise for his store in Sacramento. A thought of the convenience of having a railroad running eastward from San Francisco had, perhaps, occurred to him, and later he would build both the Central Pacific and the Southern Pacific Railroads.

People buried at Woodlawn not only came from all over the world and made their marks throughout the country, but they died in scattered locations: Thomas Nast in Ecuador, for example, Hugo Reisinger in Germany and Hideyo Noguchi in Ghana. All came to rest in Woodlawn, however, because very soon after its opening Woodlawn was recognized as "America's Père Lachaise," America's most prestigious cemetery for men and women of accomplishment. The ceremonious funeral and burial in Woodlawn accorded Admiral Farragut in 1870, attended by Farragut's comrade-in-arms President Grant himself, marked Woodlawn as a special place of national honor.

The architecture of the Gilded Age, even its funerary architecture, reflected the age's robust self-confidence. The newly-risen merchant prince or finance capitalist demanded pomp for his New York City townhouse, for his Newport or Long Island country estate, and equally for his mausoleum. It was thought only appropriate that a portion of the wealth lavished on the living should adorn the habitation of the dead. A new generation of American architects trained at Paris' École des Beaux Arts brought back classical architectural rhetoric, and the 1893 Chicago Fair validated Greece and Rome as prototypes for a new national self-image. Classical symbols such as urns, broken columns, and inverted torches, all previously an anathema to Christians, became popular in cemeteries. Various historical "revival" styles soon competed for popularity, and Egyptian, Greek and Roman, medieval Celtic and Gothic constructions jostled one another both on city streets and in cemeteries.

In 1878 the construction of mausoleums received a sudden shocking impetus when robbers stole the body of department store magnate A. T. Stewart from a Manhattan churchyard and held it for $200,000 ransom. The kidnappers eventually settled for $20,000 and surrendered the body at a secret meeting on a lonely Bronx road. Stewart was reinterred under the dome of the Garden City Cathedral in an especially sturdy vault. This ghoulish crime spurred William H. Vanderbilt to buy land on Staten Island and to build a secure private family cemetery there, but many other New York plutocrats favored suburban Woodlawn. A good share of the Society "400" chose to be buried at Woodlawn, and leading architects competed in building grandiose mausoleums for them: Hunt and Hunt; James Renwick; McKim, Mead and White; John Russell Pope and others. Woodlawn's rustic acres sprouted great temples fit for the Athenian Agora or the Roman Forum.

These constructions, however, have never overwhelmed Woodlawn's original rural landscape design. Urban architecture has come right into the carefully maintained rural environment, and the ideal compromise of extraordinary works of architecture and sculpture in a pastoral setting has been achieved perfectly. A classical temple rises beside a gentle lake on which ducks and geese glide placidly (Illustration Six). Only at Woodlawn do we really see the "rocks and rills, woods and templed hills" Baptist minister Samuel Francis Smith envisioned in "My Country 'Tis of Thee" in 1832 (Illustration Seven).

Central Park in Manhattan contrasts with Woodlawn. The Park offers a rural environment built and maintained right in the city, but kept distinct from the surrounding city. All original Central Park buildings are in rustic styles, and today we sit in Central Park's "Sheep Meadow" (where sheep actually grazed until 1934) and look over the treetops at the wall of skyscrapers surrounding the park. Woodlawn Cemetery and Central Park thus represent two different nineteenth century attempts to reconcile urban and rural environments: Woodlawn blends; Central Park excludes.

Woodlawn became a major metropolitan tourist attraction within a few years of its opening. Guidebooks and maps located the tombs of Woodlawn's famous, and the works of architecture and sculpture of special note, but the tranquil rural beauty of Woodlawn triumphs uniquely.

Gilded Age grandiosity passed like a fever early in the twentieth century, and a more restrained classicism was chosen by even the very rich. Interments at Woodlawn have continued through the twentieth century at all levels of ostentation, from the most humble to the grand. Walking through Woodlawn today, no one could argue that the splendor of anyone's tomb necessarily reflects that person's contribution to our national life. Look at the humble graves of Charles Evans Hughes, of Carrie Chapman Catt and of Ralph Bunche. Some of Woodlawn's most opulent mausoleums, by contrast, contain the remains of men and women long forgotten (Illustration Eight). Enormous wealth alone cannot ensure immortality. Woodlawn Cemetery inspires such contemplation, as it was meant to.

WOODLAWN'S LANDSCAPING

A landscape as beautiful as Woodlawn is not really "natural," but is a product of careful design. As a writer noted of Mount Auburn in 1831, "Nature under all circumstances was meant to be improved by human care; it is *unnatural* to leave it to itself; and the traces of art are never unwelcome, except when it defeats the purpose, and refuses to follow the suggestions of Nature."

Woodlawn's original acreage was about one-quarter forested back in 1863, mostly with deciduous species. The rest of the land had been farmed for generations. Philadelphia architect James C. Sidney tailored and molded this raw material to create the final beauty which we see. Sidney had had a hand in the design of several beautiful rural-type cemeteries, including Philadelphia's notable Mount Laurel Cemetery, and he had earned a widespread reputation.

ANDREW JACKSON DOWNING and ROMANTIC LANDSCAPE DESIGN

The style of landscape architecture Sidney practiced at Woodlawn was developed in America by Andrew Jackson Downing (1815-1852). Downing rejected putting

Nature into a strait jacket of formal geometric shapes, as the French and Italians did in their gardens, but followed English landscape taste in preferring an "irregular" style. The contrast between the irregular, or "Romantic" style, and the formal style is well demonstrated by the contrast between Woodlawn and the formal palace grounds at Versailles in France, or in the formal city of Washington, D.C., which was planned by a native of Versailles.

The basic elements of Romantic landscape design include winding paths, a balance between open vistas and more heavily wooded scenes and rolling topography. Each turn in a path ought to surprise a visitor with a picturesque composition. Trees and shrubs are planted to frame certain views and to serve as backdrops to other features. Lakes and ponds reflect the sky and the moonlight, while a babbling brook is Nature's own voice. Woodlawn's lake feeds a brook, spanned by an arched stone bridge, which runs down to the Bronx River (Illustration Nine).

Downing believed that our behavior is affected by our environment, and that such a pastoral landscape has a calming effect. Therefore Downing eagerly joined William Cullen Bryant when Bryant began lobbying for a public park in New York City. Downing did not live to see Central Park completed. He died in a tragic boating accident when he was only thirty-seven years old, but Downing had been a friend and teacher of Frederick Olmsted, and he had been responsible for bringing Calvert Vaux, the park's codesigner, over to America from England.

Golf courses continue the American art of pastoral landscape architecture which our cemeteries began and our parks followed. Rolling topography, winding paths, the sound of wind through trees, irregularly placed roughs, sandtraps, and water courses are all derived from Romantic landscape ideas, and so is the very idea that it is beneficial to be out in such a Natural setting.

America's first permanent golf club, the Saint Andrew's Golf Club, was founded in Yonkers, just a couple of miles from Woodlawn. Scotland-born John Reid (1840-1916) introduced the game in 1888, and he let his friends practice out in his cow pasture through the summer. A dinner at Reid's house on November 14, 1888, marked the club's official organization with Reid as president. Reid is recognized as "the father of golf in America." He is interred at Woodlawn, and he would undoubtedly be pleased to know that a popular public course has been built across the street from Woodlawn, a good woodshot from where he lies.

THE CHOICE OF TREES

Landscape architects consider the placement of each tree and shrub carefully; the original distribution of plants is not just "left alone." Variations of size and shape among plants must be composed in order to provide pleasing views as the visitor moves through the design. Some species of trees are tall and thin, others broader. Short trees are planted to stand in front of taller trees when seen from selected spots. Trees and shrubs must be arranged to frame the stone memorials and mausoleums. Also, different species are most lush during different periods of the year, and the designer wants the visual balance to shift through the months, but always to be interesting. In cemeteries the distribution of evergreens is especially important in order to prevent the cemetery's ever looking too barren and depressing. And what colors are the trees? If you think that green is just one color, look through the following pages at the placement of different shades of green to delight the eye. Woodlawn also offers rich distribution of red trees: Japanese elms and maples. Flowering trees and shrubs—dogwood, magnolia, azalea—blossom one after the other through the spring, so that each visit to the cemetery from week to week reveals new beauty.

Trees have not only decorative value, but they have symbolic value as well. All deciduous trees, for example, are supposed to remind us of the Resurrection. The acacia tree is said to have supplied Christ's thorny crown. An oak tree symbolizes "steadfast faith." The book of *I Kings* XIX, 4, tells us that Elijah wanted to lie down and die under a juniper tree. Any "weeping" species is especially appropriate for a cemetery. The cypress tree is too, for Greek mythology relates that when the god Apollo's mortal friend Cyparissus died, Apollo transformed his lifeless body into the cypress tree. Cypress trees should forever stand guard beside the graves of those who were much loved in life. These stories may seem obscure to us today, but the symbolic language of trees and flowers was fairly common knowledge among our Victorian ancestors. The various trees in the cemetery spoke to the visitors.

Individual fine trees invite appreciation. Downing believed that a single noble tree is "more beautiful than Grecian Apollo itself," and naturalist Wilson Flagg suggested that trees should replace gravestones, for as men advance in civilization, he wrote, they "prize nature more and art less." This custom does prevail in parts of the Mideast, and an echo of it can be seen in the Whitney family plot at Woodlawn. Wilson Flaggs' grandnephew, James Montgomery Flagg (1877-1960), the man who designed America's famous World War I poster "Uncle Sam wants you!" rests at Woodlawn under a lovely tree with a simple gravestone.

In 1985 the New York City Parks Department designated the 113 most beautiful trees in New York City; five of these are in Woodlawn. These include a European cut-leaf beech, a weeping beech (in front of the Gould mausoleum), a white pine, a pendent silver linden (Illustration Ten), and an umbrella pine. None of these is native to the area; all were planted to beautify. A 1960 survey of shade trees in Woodlawn listed 3,388, and this did not include any of the ornamental flowering trees abundant throughout the cemetery, nor the Japanese maples, both weeping and upright, or the unusual specimens such as golden rain trees, hackberry, katsura, silver bell, Kentucky coffee trees and cork trees. A massive white oak is probably the oldest tree in Woodlawn. About 225 years old, it stands 75 feet high and boasts a girth of 14½ feet and a spread of 100 feet. The American tradition of a cemetery as an arboretum, begun at Mount Auburn in 1831, is carried on magnificently at Woodlawn.

WOODLAWN TODAY

Today Woodlawn is not only one of the most beautiful open spaces in New York City, but also a site of continuing interments. The beauty of the markers and monuments, however, never overwhelms that of the landscaping, which is conscientiously maintained by a staff which reaches 200 in the summer. The diverse trees and shrubs, especially the flowering species, present a fresh display each week from early spring through late fall. The photographs in this book have been taken through the course of a year. The cemetery's grounds offer a natural sanctuary to both migrating birds and those permanently in residence. Over one hundred species have been spotted at Woodlawn, including the rare Eastern kingbird, the white-eyed virio and the yellow-billed flycatcher. Some thirty-five to forty Canada geese and a colony of mallard ducks make Woodlawn their home. George B. Grinnell (1849-1938), who organized the first Audubon Society and who is buried at Woodlawn, would approve.

A visitor to Woodlawn notices that many plots are specially tended and provided with fresh flowers not only by families, but by groups and associations. This is distinctively American. We commemorate our past collectively. The New York Press Club has remembered Nellie Bly, and other graves show the continuing remembrance of Masons, the Y.M.C.A, various military units, War Mothers, and other organizations. Some military units, churches and other groups hold plots for their members' eventual need.

Politicians fare less well. The graves of the six New York City mayors and of the one Brooklyn mayor buried at Woodlawn receive no official care, nor do those of the numerous members of the United States House of Representatives, or of the three United States senators (who represented Colorado, Montana, and Nevada, but not New York), of the eight United States cabinet secretaries (including Benjamin Butler, the only man ever to hold two cabinet positions at the same time), of the first man to hold the title of Solicitor General (Benjamin Bristow 1832-1896; he also served as Secretary of the Treasury), or that of the United States Supreme Court Chief Justice, Charles Evans Hughes. All these are especially decorated only by family, or are maintained normally by the Woodlawn Association. I should note that no graves or monuments were tampered with or decorated for the photographs in this book. All were photographed as they were found, with any fresh flowers or flags left by anonymous tenders.

Although Phoebe Underhill has been joined by almost 300,000 neighbors since her interment, that first one in 1865, cemetery space is not closed. By the mid-1970's, however, all but twenty-nine of the cemetery's four hundred acres had been sold or developed as roads or landscaping. Remaining open areas were surveyed to determine which were suitable for ground burials and which could not serve that purpose because of the thinness of the soil on underlying bedrock. These areas were set aside for community mausoleums. A community mausoleum contains multiple crypts available individually, as compared with private mausoleums for single or family occupancy. A series of adjacent crypts can insure family propinquity just as family plots always have. New Yorkers as distinguished as Robert Moses (1888-1981), the city planner whose work had enormous impact across America, have chosen these community facilities. The community mausoleums may remind us of the arcaded galleries of Genoa's Staglieno Cemetery, but at Woodlawn we are never far from Nature—just a glance out the door or window reminds us.

As cremation has been increasingly accepted, a crematory has been added to Woodlawn's facilities. The crematory is in Woolworth Chapel, a nonsectarian chapel which was given to the cemetery by Mrs. Frederick Woolworth (Illustration Ten). Frederick Woolworth was a distant cousin of Frank, the founder of the five-and-dime chain. Frederick headed the English Woolworth's for many years. Woodlawn has also constructed a columbarium for the preservation of urns containing the ashes of the dead. With these facilities Woodlawn Cemetery can continue to serve for many years, and in fact, a number of living Americans as famous as any discussed in this book have already expressed their intention to be buried at Woodlawn.

14

Illustration Five: Urban development pressed up to the gates of Woodlawn and swept on to the North, but the Cemetery preserved a peaceful environment. Visitors enjoy feeding Woodlawn's tame ducks from along the lakeshore.

Illustration Six: Rural and urban blend peaceably at Woodlawn, as here, where ducks glide placidly by a lakeside classical temple. The Warner family controlled the International Phosphate Company.

Illustration Seven: In "My Country 'Tis of Thee" Baptist minister Samuel Francis Smith envisioned America as a land of "rocks and rills, woods and templed hills." Smith's vision seems realized at Woodlawn, where the Sterling family mausoleum, designed by Stanford White as a Doric temple, crowns a hill. The rill (brook) visible among the rocks in the lower right corner tumbles down to the Bronx River. John W. Sterling (1844-1918) was a founder of the prominent New York law firm of Shearman and Sterling.

Illustration Eight: John H. Harbeck (1839-1910) inherited a Brooklyn real estate fortune and then increased it through shrewd investments in Colorado. Architect Theodore E. Blake built this magnificent mausoleum for him. If the power company would ever agree to run a wire to it, the electric lighting fixtures would work, and an electric music box would play masses.

Illustration Nine: Woodlawn's 400 acres straddle the crest separating the watersheds of the Hudson and the Bronx Rivers, and the stream from Woodlawn's lake tumbles down through the Cemetery to the Bronx River.

Illustration Ten: Woodlawn's nondenominational chapel was a bequest of Mrs. Fred Woolworth. Architect Robertson Ward designed it in a modern adaptation of the colonial style, and it was dedicated at an inter-faith service in 1936. Its copper-covered steeple rises 130 feet. The two trees visible to the right here were among those designated "Great Trees of New York City" in 1985: the pendent silver linden (Tilia petiolaris) with the yellowing leaves in the foreground and the white pine (Pinus strobus) to the far right.

THE INDIVIDUAL GRAVES TREATED IN THIS BOOK

Almost 300,000 people have been interred at Woodlawn since 1865. Several, such as F. W. Woolworth, were household names when they died, and their fame has survived them. Others, such as Herman Melville, were obscure when they died, but have since been remembered. Still others were famous in their own day, but have since been forgotten. A sample of graves of interesting and important people has been selected for this book (Illustration Eleven).

I based my selections on several criteria. My first and overriding criterion was that each of the people featured here made a contribution to our *national* life and culture. Each made American history; several made world history. To have been important in New York alone is not enough to be included. There are many famous New Yorkers in Woodlawn whose achievements in that city, however great, did not have significant effect outside New York. Of the six New York City mayors buried at Woodlawn, for example, only Fiorello LaGuardia is singled out here. This is not only because he made New York a national showplace for urban social programs, but also because of his earlier roles in World War I and in Congress.

Not everyone profiled here was an American citizen. Exclusionary federal legislation prevented Orientals from becoming naturalized Americans from the late nineteenth century until well into the twentieth, and any American citizen who married an Oriental immediately surrendered American citizenship. Therefore neither Doctor Jokichi Takamine nor Doctor Hideyo Noguchi, two of the most famous men in this volume, and both of whom spent most of their lives in the United States, married Americans, and made important contributions to America, ever became an American citizen. Vernon Castle never surrendered his English citizenship, although he died in Texas on an Allied training mission during World War I.

The fact that each of the people discussed in this book had a national or international impact does not necessarily mean that each name was famous in the person's own lifetime, or is even immediately recognizable today. Several would never have made the cover of any of today's celebrity magazines, but their contributions were nevertheless significant. When I began my research I had never heard of Judge Addison Brown, of Michael Pupin, or of Carrie Chapman Catt, and I wonder how many readers have, but now I know that we live in a world they made, and their stories are fascinating.

Another criterion was that each individual's impact must have endured. Many entertainers' fame in particular has faded away. Florence Mills (1895-1927), "the Blackbird of Harlem," was one of the greatest stars of her day, but few remember her now, or any of the songs that were her signatures. James K. Hackett (1869-1926), created on the American stage in the 1890's the very type of the dashing hero with cloak and sword, an archetype that survived into the film era. His Paris production of *Macbeth* won him the ribbon of Chevalier de la Légion d'Honneur, as his tombstone proudly proclaims to largely indifferent passersby today. Our critical appraisal of artists rises and falls. F. Hopkinson Smith (1838-1915) and A. F. Tait (1819-1905) were well-known artists in their day, but today both men are considered only minor. The section "Other Notables" lists many of these famous people not singled out for fullscale individual treatment.

I have tried to include a variety of fields of endeavor and so the list of, for exam-

Illustration Eleven: Not all Woodlawn memorials are to single individuals. Mrs. Anna Bliss (1851-1935) dedicated this one to all those who lost their lives in the sinking of the Titanic *in 1912. The over-lifesize figures were created by sculptor Robert Aitken, who also carved the west pediment of the Supreme Court building in Washington. The quotation on the great curving bench, "Our souls have sight of that immortal sea which brought us hither," is from Wordsworth. Mrs. Bliss is interred in a crypt cut into the back of the monument. Her daughter and son-in-law, Mr. and Mrs. Robert Woods Bliss, were to have been interred here also, but they chose instead to be interred on the grounds of Dumbarton Oaks, Washington's beautiful museum and international conference center which the Blisses gave to Harvard University.*

ple, prominent financiers had to be trimmed to allow perhaps another athlete or musician. I often had to choose among people whose careers or achievements were similar. The mausoleums of J. C. Penney (1875-1971), F. W. Woolworth (1852-1919), and Samuel Kress (1863-1955) are around the corner from each other at Woodlawn, as their stores are in towns across America, but I have chosen to illustrate only Woolworth's.

Visual interest was a last consideration in narrowing the selection. Many of the greatest individuals lie in simple graves. Many others, however, have beautiful monuments, and I have tried to show the diversity of these. Both Louis Sherry (1856-1926) and Charles Delmonico (1860-1902) are interred at Woodlawn; both names are synonymous with fine food. They operated competing restaurants; they both educated American tastes, featured American raw materials, developed new dishes, and refined a distinctively American cuisine and diet. Charles Delmonico lies under a simple cross, while Louis Sherry ordered a fine mausoleum designed by prominent architect Stanford White.

Among the 300,000 names in Woodlawn's central file are perhaps still more famous people whose names would be recognizable if I had thought of looking for them, but one cannot think of every interesting possibility. Days and weeks spent exploring the cemetery grounds still cannot discover every interesting history buried there, and I don't know every name important in American history anyway. Each time I walked through the cemetery with another friend whose interests are different from mine, he or she would notice a name on a stone and ask, "Oh! Is that *the* So-and-so?" And each time sent me scurrying to reference books to learn about an important person of whom I had never heard before! There may well be more high ranking government officials interred at Woodlawn than those senators and cabinet secretaries I numbered above, but I didn't discover them. Addison Brown, Finley Peter Dunne, Joseph Leyendecker, Madam C. J. Walker and Walt Kuhn are just a few of the names I discovered simply while wandering through Woodlawn. The fact that they are interred there had not been publicly noted before.

Here then is my gallery of makers of American history at Woodlawn. You are welcome to visit and compile your own.

23

ARCHIPENKO

ALEXANDER (1887-1964)

Alexander Archipenko approached and solved more aesthetic problems than any other twentieth century sculptor, and he expressed them in more different ways. "Sculptures," he wrote, "are lucrative for the imagination, and it is only through imagination that we can build a civilization."

He was born in Kiev, but moved to Paris in 1908, and there he and his friends Picasso and Braque created the cubist art movement. Archipenko experimented with simplified geometric forms, as illustrated here with "The Gondolier" (1914). He even turned sculpture inside-out, substituting hollows for solid forms. "I draw a parallel," he wrote, "between space problems and the pause in music, which has as much meaning as sound." He colored his sculptures, combined materials, and even motorized some of them, which he called "changing paintings." From the school and studio which he established in New York after becoming an American citizen in 1929, his sculpture and graphic arts exercised world-wide influence.

ANGELICA (1893-1957)

Angelica Bruno-Schmitz was a noted sculptor when she married Alexander Archipenko in 1921, and she continued her own teaching and sculpting career through their years together. When she predeceased him, he chose to place a work of hers on their Woodlawn plot.

HERMAN (1837-1901)

Meatpacker Herman Armour lies in this grand mausoleum designed by architect James Renwick, famous for Saint Patrick's Cathedral in New York and the Smithsonian "Castle" building in Washington, D.C. The bronze dome is cast in a classical pattern of scales, and the pink granite reminds some observers of a ham.

The Armour family once controlled so much of America's grain and meat supplies that the "Meat Trust" joined Standard Oil and other industry concentrations as targets for political attack. Herman had been the first of the six Armour brothers from upstate New York to head west and to start the family's food company.

BENJAMIN T. (1809-1889)

Benjamin T. Babbitt's soap was one of America's first nationally advertised consumer products, and because Babbitt's soap was sold from brightly painted street carts loaded with musicians, the phrase "get on the bandwagon" entered our language. Babbitt was also the first manufacturer to give free samples to introduce new products and the first to advertise his factory as a tourist attraction. By marketing his soaps, baking powder and baking soda in a variety of convenient and eye-catching packages, Babbitt gave birth to the packaging and design styles which compete for our attention in supermarkets today. His name became a household word from coast to coast, and in 1922 Sinclair Lewis adopted it for the title character of his bestseller about a vulgar, enthusiastic businessman.

Babbitt was also a prolific inventor, and he registered 104 patents on products ranging from soaps and cosmetics to pumps and engines, railroad cars, armaments, and fire extinguishers. His immense wealth got him into trouble with America's first income tax, which was introduced during the Civil War. The government claimed that Babbitt owed $150,000, but eventually settled for $20,000.

This monumental sarcophagus marks Benjamin T. Babbitt's Woodlawn plot. Sarcophagi were always used for the actual interment in antiquity, but here in America we often adopt the form purely as a monument. The Babbitts lie in front of it. The plot overlooks the Bronx River Valley and slopes down behind the sarcophagus.

JULES (1861-1944)

Stockbroker Jules Bache collected art works formerly owned by kings and Medici princes, and he wanted nothing less than a pharoah's mausoleum. Egyptian mythology explains why architect John Russell Pope patterned Bache's mausoleum on the Temple of Isis, which stands on the Island of Phylae in the Nile River.

Seth, the god of violence, murdered his brother Osiris, the sun god. Osiris' faithful wife, Isis, secretly bore Osiris a posthumous son, Horus. When Horus grew to manhood he overpowered his uncle Seth, resurrected his father Osiris, and appointed Osiris to rule the underworld. Egyptians believed that when each pharoah died he assimilated to Osiris, and the pharoah's son and successor ruled as "the living Horus." This pre-Christian story of a god who died like a man and was resurrected to eternal life spread throughout the ancient world and paved the way for Christianity.

Isis' temple, a rectangle with great columns carved as papyrus, represents the cradle in which Osiris was reborn as Horus/pharoah, and so it is sometimes called the pharoah's cradle. The winged eye above the lintel is the form in which Horus flew into the sky in order to detect the lurking Seth. Osiris decreed that this symbol should always protect temple doorways, and it can be seen at Woodlawn on the Bache, Woolworth, and other Egyptian-style mausoleums.

After Oliver Belmont's death, Alva devoted herself to women's suffrage. She served as President of the National Women's Party, which still today campaigns for the Equal Rights Amendment from its headquarters building, donated by Alva, just behind the Supreme Court in Washington. Women presided at Alva's funeral, and in the Belmont mausoleum hangs her suffragette banner: "Failure is impossible."

OLIVER HAZARD PERRY (1858-1908) and his wife
ALVA SMITH VANDERBILT (1853-1933)

This stunning mausoleum is a copy of the chapel of Saint Hubert, a masterpiece of late fifteenth-century French architecture which overlooks the Loire Valley from a terrace high above the city of Amboise. The original is the final resting place of Leonardo da Vinci; this copy is the final resting place of Mr. and Mrs. Oliver Belmont.

Oliver Hazard Perry Belmont bore the name of his great uncle, the hero of the 1813 Battle of Lake Erie ("We have met the enemy, and they are ours!"), and he was the grandson of the Commodore Perry who "opened" Japan. Oliver Belmont himself graduated from Annapolis and served in the navy, but then followed his father, August Belmont, into banking. He took time out from that only to serve one term in Congress.

Oliver's wife, Alva Belmont, had previously been married to William Vanderbilt, who had commissioned architect Richard Morris Hunt to build for her a grand French renaissance chateau on Fifth Avenue and the magnificent Marble House in Newport, Rhode Island. Alva switched husbands, but she remained true to her preference in architecture, and she commissioned Hunt's sons to build this mausoleum.

The choice of a chapel dedicated to Saint Hubert, the patron saint of hunting, reflects Oliver Belmont's passion for horses. Belmont Racetrack and the Belmont Stakes were family interests. Saint Hubert's legend is recounted on the lintel. He was a worldly young man out hunting on a Good Friday when a stag bearing a crucifix between its antlers appeared and converted him to Christianity. The lintel also shows Saints Anthony and Christopher. In the tympanum King Charles VIII and his wife, Anne of Brittany, kneel before the Virgin and Child.

NELLIE (1864-1922)
(Elizabeth Cochrane Seaman)

America cheered when the intrepid 22-year-old reporter Nellie Bly set out to best the fictional Phileas Fogg's record trip "Around the World in Eighty Days." Her employer Joseph Pulitzer front-paged her dispatches detailing her perilous journey, and over a million newspaper readers entered a contest to guess exactly how long it would take Nellie to get back to New York. She made it in 72 days, 6 hours, 11 minutes and 14 seconds, even having stopped to interview Fogg's creator Jules Verne in France along her way. Verne had wished her luck, but doubted that she could beat Fogg's time.

Nellie Bly pioneered investigative journalism, exposing abuses in politics and employment and official dereliction of duty in hospitals and prisons. Born Elizabeth Cochrane, she took her pen name from the heroine of Stephen Foster's popular song, in which Nellie "wields a broom to sweep the kitchen clean." She always sought the "inside story." Her first series of articles revealed the grim conditions for women working in factories, and later she feigned insanity to get herself committed to an asylum. By pre-arrangement, friends won her release after ten days, and her articles on that experience prompted more humane treatment of the institutionalized mentally ill.

She died destitute, and her grave was unmarked until 1978. In that year the New York Press Club, prodded by Woodlawn, formally recognized Nellie's leading role in her profession.

GAIL (1801- 1874)

Inventor Gail Borden surveys the Bronx River Valley from his perch atop a tall column. The document in his right hand may be Texas' 1836 Declaration of Independence from Mexico, or the new Republic's Constitution, both of which Borden helped write, or perhaps it's the plans for Houston, for Galveston, or for any of the other Texas cities Borden laid out. The column's base condenses the story of Borden's later efforts to condense milk, "I tried and failed. I tried again and again and succeeded."

Among Gail Borden's many inventions was this "terraqueous machine," a sail-driven prairie schooner for land and sea. At its first demonstration on Galveston beach it sailed into the water all right, but capsized and dumped its passengers.

BROWN

Judge Brown oversaw the construction of the New York Botanical Garden's most spectacular building, this crystal palace conservatory patterned after the one at Kew Gardens outside London. Each of this building's eleven pavilions creates a different environment for plants, and the elaborate complex covers an acre. The central dome is ninety feet high and one hundred feet in diameter. Judge Brown's resting place at Woodlawn is just a couple of miles to the North.

ADDISON (1830-1913)

Judge Addison Brown's college roommate and pal, Horatio Alger, might well have written the Judge's own successful life story. At sixteen Brown suffered through the humiliation of family bankruptcy and the disappointment of having his own wages withheld by his employer, a creditor of his father's. At the time of his death, however, he was financially comfortable and had earned distinction in two separate "careers." He was not only one of the most respected jurists in America, but also a world famous botanist, founder of the New York Botanical Garden, and working on a second edition of his monumental *Illustrated Flora of the Northern United States, Canada, and the British Possessions*, which is still a standard scientific reference work.

Judge Brown's monument is a sculptural copy of the sarcophagus of the Roman general Cornelius Scipio Barbatus (d. 298 B.C.). The original in the Vatican Museum was reproduced and adapted widely in the nineteenth century. One can be seen at Père Lachaise (Illustration One), and Woodlawn has several like it.

The Arab-Israeli Armistice which Ralph Bunche negotiated in 1949, and for which he won the Nobel Peace Prize in 1950, lasted until the Arab-Israeli War of 1967. Here Bunche shakes hands with David Ben-Gurion, Israel's first premier (1949 to 1953, and again 1955 to 1963), watched by Trygve Lie, the United Nations' first Secretary General (1946 to 1953).

RALPH (1904-1971)

The olive branch of peace appropriately marks the resting place of Ralph Bunche, winner of the Nobel Peace Prize in 1950 and the Presidential Medal of Freedom, our nation's highest civilian honor, in 1963.

Bunche was born in poverty and worked his way through the University of California as a janitor. During World War II he entered the United States Office of Strategic Services, and by 1946 he had become the State Department's expert on colonial affairs. In 1948 he went to assist Count Bernadotte of Sweden mediate an end to the Arab-Israeli War over Palestine, and when Bernadotte was assassinated, Bunche worked on alone, despite the belligerents' refusal to face each other over a bargaining table. He eventually negotiated an armistice among seven Arab states and Israel. Through the following years his diplomatic skills were put to good use in the Suez, Katanga, Kashmir and Cyprus. He retired as Undersecretary General of the United Nations in 1971, the year of his death.

"I have," he wrote, "a number of very strong biases. I have a deep-seated bias against hate and intolerance. I have a bias against racial and religious bigotry. I have a bias against war, a bias for peace. I have a bias which leads me to believe in the essential goodness of my fellow man."

Benjamin Franklin Butler and his wife, Harriet, are seated in the front row of this 1846 family daguerreotype which was made to send to William when he was away at school. Benjamin had just declined President Polk's offer to resume the office of Secretary of War, but he continued to serve as United States Attorney for the Southern District of New York.

BENJAMIN FRANKLIN (1795-1858)

Benjamin Franklin Butler was the only American ever to hold two cabinet offices simultaneously; both Secretary of War and Attorney General under Andrew Jackson. Butler later founded New York University Law School, and at the end of his life he successfully defended a Jewish officer against ouster from the United States Navy, for the first time publicly identifying anti-Semiticism as a force in American life. Butler was originally buried in a downtown Manhattan churchyard, but later reinterred here at Woodlawn behind the new family plot marker.

WILLIAM A. (1825-1902)

Benjamin's son, William A. Butler, won early acclaim for a poetic parody of New York society ladies, "Nothing to Wear," and the success of that joke dogged him all through a distinguished career as lawyer, historian, novelist and, yes, poet.

WILLIAM A., II (1853 -1923)

Benjamin's grandson, another William Butler, followed in the family tradition as a prominent New York attorney.

35

Gilbert Seldes described Irene Castle dancing, "There were no steps, no tricks or stunts. There was only dancing, and it was all that one ever dreamed of flight, with wings poised, and swooping down gently to rest."

VERNON (1887-1918) and his wife, IRENE (1893-1969)

Dance team Vernon and Irene Castle rest beneath this lovely peristyle which Irene had constructed when Vernon lost his life in World War I. Irene later placed here Sally Farnham's sculpture "The End of the Day," which Miss Farnham modeled after a tired member of Isadora Duncan's dance troupe.

Miss Hay, in the light dress in the center, and Mrs. Catt, directly behind the bouquet, receive congratulations upon their return to New York from the Washington ceremonies surrounding ratification of the 19th amendment. To the left stands New York State Governor, Alfred E. Smith.

CARRIE CHAPMAN (1859-1947)

Carrie Chapman Catt replaced Susan B. Anthony as president of the National American Woman Suffrage Association in 1900. "I feel the honor of this position," she said, "much less than its responsibility." At the time women could vote in only four states (Wyoming, Colorado, Utah and Idaho), but Mrs. Catt brilliantly led the campaign which achieved ratification of the 19th amendment to the Constitution, guaranteeing women's suffrage across the country, in 1920.

HAY

MARY GARRETT (1857-1928)

Mary Garrett Hay led the late nineteenth century temperance movement, but at the turn of the century she took up woman suffrage, and assumed the presidency of the New York State Woman's Suffrage Party. Miss Hay lived with Mrs. Catt after the death of Mrs. Catt's husband in 1905, and she preceded Mrs. Catt in death in 1928.

WILLIAM A. (1839-1925)

Senator William A. Clark of Montana insisted that he was a resident of Butte, but his 130-room mansion on Fifth Avenue in New York was so gaudily spectacular that one satirist wrote:

> Senator Copper of Tonapah Ditch
> Made a clean billion in minin' and sich,
> Hiked fer Noo York, where his money he blew
> Buildin' a palace on Fift' Avenoo.
> "How," sez the Senator, "can I look proudest?
> Build me a house that'll holler the loudest."

The house was filled with art treasures which make up the heart of the Corcoran Gallery of Art in Washington, D.C. today, but the great mansion came down only two years after the Senator's death and interment at Woodlawn.

Senator Clark had once been listed as "one of a hundred men who own America." He held mines, smelters and banks in Montana and Arizona; railroads, timberlands and cattle ranches throughout the West, and plantations in Mexico to supply sugar to his refineries in Los Angeles, where he had vast real estate holdings. Because he owned everything alone and outright, no one will ever be able to calculate the immensity of his fortune.

His first election to the United States Senate miscarried when the Senate refused to seat him, and his second election was declared "null and void on account of briberies, attempted briberies, and corrupt practices," but Montana sent him back a third time, and he sat from 1901 to 1907.

Senator Clark's Woodlawn mausoleum is a bit more restrained than his Fifth Avenue mansion, but it certainly is grand.

A collection of Cohans appeared onstage in George's *George Washington, Jr.*, to sing "It's a Grand Old Flag" on February 12, 1906. George holds the flag. Jerry and Helen Cohan, George's parents, are second and third in from the left. At stage right, seated and wearing a huge white hat, is George's wife at the time, Ethel Levey.

GEORGE M. (1878-1942)

George M. Cohan, his parents, and his sister Josephine Cohan Niblo, who once toured in vaudeville as "The Four Cohans," reunited in death in this Louis C. Tiffany-designed mausoleum. A flag is always in the door, placed there by a veterans' group which remembers George's special Congressional Medal of Honor for having written "It's a Grand Old Flag." During Cohan's funeral the organ at Saint Patrick's Cathedral for the first time played a secular song, "Over There," at a funeral march tempo.

LOTTA (1847-1924)

When eight-year-old Lotta Crabtree first sang and danced on a crude barroom stage in a California mining town, appreciative miners showered her with gold dust. For the next 36 years her onstage turns, her pantomimes and skits full of warmth and good humour beguiled audiences across America. By the time she retired in 1891, she was easily the most popular—and the richest—entertainer in America.

Lotta had earned the love of crowds, but, as with many later child movie stars, her personal life was protected and lonely. She retired into seclusion so totally that when she died many people were astonished that she had so recently been alive. Nostalgic editorials, as in the *New York Times*, wondered "How did 'La Petite Lotta' get to be 77? This was the Immortal Child." A few days later front pages blazoned that she had left her millions for the care of disabled World War I veterans. In 1951, actress Mitzi Gaynor starred in a film biography of Lotta, "Golden Girl."

At Woodlawn Lotta rests beside her mother and her aunt, Charlotte Vernon, who represented Lotta at the 1875 dedication of Lotta's gift to the people of San Francisco, an elaborate iron fountain which is today a San Francisco historic landmark. The fountain never failed to provide water during the San Francisco earthquake and fire of 1906, and so each year it is the site of the memorial service to those who lost their lives; the service begins each April 18 at 5:18 a.m. Lotta is remembered anonymously here at Woodlawn.

Howard Lindsay and Russel Crouse successfully dramatized Day's reminiscences, and the 1945 Broadway cast shown here starred Wallis Clark and Lily Cahill. The film version with William Powell and Irene Dunne appeared in 1947, but movie censors absurdly clipped Father's famous exit line, "I'm going to be baptized, damn it!"

CLARENCE (1874-1935)

"Life With Father," based on the autobiographical sketches of Clarence Day, holds the record for continuous performances of a non-musical play on Broadway. The play's focus, irascible Mr. Day's refusal to be baptized, was only one of many reminiscences which together constitute a genial portrayal of a mercurial father forever outsmarted by his clever but affectionate wife.

The Days were, in fact, a solid upper-class family. Clarence, Sr. (1844-1927) was a respected stockbroker, for many years a governor of the New York Stock Exchange; his father Benjamin (1810-1889) had founded the New York *Sun* in 1833, and his brother Benjamin (1838-1916), invented an important engraving process.

Young Clarence retired to a sickbed when crippled by arthritis at the age of 29, but his affliction never soured his view of life. His satirical writings always surrendered their sting to an extraordinary sympathy and understanding. His first book, *This Simian World* (1920), interprets human traits as the natural result of our having descended from monkeys, and speculates on what we would be like had we descended from other animals. Had we descended from bees or ants, for instance, we would have been industrious, but apolitical and without sufficient self-consciousness and reason; from felines, fearless, suave, clean and resolute, but less capable of friendship, and so on through the animal kingdom. Day's autobiographical sketches were collected in *God and My Father* (1932), and *Life With Father* (1935), upon which the play was based, but the Day monument at Woodlawn seems to illustrate Clarence's posthumous collection, *Life With Mother* (1937).

In *Life With Father* Day wrote, "Mother used to go to the Cemetery in Woodlawn with her arms full of flowers and lay the pretty things by some headstone, as a sign of remembrance . . . Father refused. Positively. He winked robustly at me and said, 'I'll be going there soon enough!'" And so he did. Clarence, Sr. died in 1927, and his son joined him at Woodlawn in 1935.

DeLAMATER

This 1863 print illustrates the battle between the ironclads *Monitor* and *Merrimac*. The day before this battle the *Merrimac* had sunk one Union battleship and crippled two others blockading Hampton Roads, but on Sunday morning, March 9, 1862, when she came out to finish off the Union fleet, she was met by the *Monitor*, just down from New York. For four hours the two ironclads slugged it out, but neither was able to do much damage to the other. At the end of the day the *Merrimac's* withdrawal to Norfolk was an effective victory for the Union blockade. The *London Times* moaned "Whereas we had one hundred and forty-nine first class warships, we have now two [iron-broadsided ships]. There is not a ship in the English Navy apart from those two that it would not be madness to trust to an engagement with that little *Monitor*."

CORNELIUS (1821-1889)

The ball atop Cornelius DeLamater's monument might well represent the cannonballs which bounced off the sides of the *Monitor*, which DeLamater designed and built with his friend, Jon Ericsson. The *Monitor* stopped the *Merrimac* at Hampton Roads, Virginia, on March 9, 1862, in history's first battle between ironclads. During the battle, DeLamater's own civilian employees actually operated the *Monitor's* boilers and turret machinery; these men later returned to their jobs in New York as if it had been all in a day's work!

DeLamater went on to invent and manufacture firefighting pumps, engines, industrial presses, mechanical refrigeration equipment, hydraulic stage machinery, and the great gun which shoots "the human cannonball" at the circus—it's actually a spring. In 1881 DeLamater built the world's first successful submarine torpedo boat.

THE FUNERAL PROCESSION PASSING THE CITY HALL, NEW YORK.—Drawn by Taylor and Meeker.

Ceremonies for the re-interment of the members of the De Long Arctic Expedition included a naval review in New York harbor, ceremonies at the Brooklyn Navy Yard, and a solemn procession up Broadway. The bodies had lain in Siberia under a driftwood spar cross erected by their comrades. A copy of this, a great stone cross with marble icicles atop a granite cairn, stands today across the Severn River from the United States Naval Academy at Annapolis. (*Harper's Weekly*, March 1, 1884.)

LT. COMMANDER GEORGE WASHINGTON (1844-1881)

The De Long Islands just north of Siberia were named to commemorate the tragic Arctic expedition of Lt. Commander George W. De Long. The expedition sailed from San Francisco in 1879 in an effort to reach the North Pole, but scarcely two months after leaving port the ship was trapped in ice. She drifted helplessly to the Northwest for twenty-one months before the ice finally crushed and sank her. The men then set out by sledges and small boats to the South toward Siberia, but, ultimately, only thirteen of the thirty-three expedition members survived. De Long himself was among those who perished in the ice and snow.

Survivors of the expedition returned to Siberia in 1882 to find and bury their fallen comrades, but the bodies were not to rest there long. Americans were so moved by the tragedy of these brave men's courage that the United States government sent another expedition to return the bodies to America, and they were re-interred with naval honors here at Woodlawn, not far from Admiral Farragut.

From the tragedy of the De Long Expedition scientists did learn much about the geography of the Far North and about Arctic Ocean currents.

DILLON

SIDNEY (1812-1892)

Sidney Dillon's long bushy sideburns identify him in the front row among Union Pacific executives at ceremonies marking the completion of the transcontinental railroad at Promontory Point, Utah, on May 10, 1869. He stands on the ground to the right of the tracks and ties. The next day trains began running regularly over the entire line from New York to San Francisco, and, Dillon wrote, "a new empire had been thrown open in the heart of a continent." Dillon kept one of the ceremonial silver spikes on his desk until his death.

Sidney Dillon, who built the transcontinental Union Pacific Railroad, chose to mark his Woodlawn plot with a distinctive Celtic cross. Hundreds of these crosses, some of them as old as 1,200 years, still dot Ireland and the surrounding islands. Each is covered with fine carving, and the circle at the crossing of the arms represents God's unity and completeness. Woodlawn boasts many of these crosses, several of which are reproductions of specific prototypes in Ireland, although few are as tall as Dillon's. The pattern of interlacing on Dillon's, representing eternity, and of knobs, called bossels, seems to be based on the South Cross at the medieval Monastery of Clonmacnois.

DuCHAILLU

This charming vignette illustrates DuChaillu's book, *The Country of the Dwarfs* (1872), detailing his experiences among the pygmies of West Africa.

PAUL (1835-1903)

Paul DuChaillu ignited one of the most explosive scientific controversies of the nineteenth century. When he published reports describing what he had seen during an expedition in West Africa — the gorillas and other large apes, and the human pygmies — his discoveries seemed the most fantastic ever reported. Distinguished scholars condemned his writings as gross absurdities, exaggerations and lies. The Philadelphia Academy of Natural Sciences, however, which had financed his expedition, stood behind him and even financed a second expedition. Eventually, of course, everything he had written was proven true, and today the mountains of the West African country of Gabon bear DuChaillu's name.

DuChaillu spent much of his later life exploring and writing about the northernmost reaches of Europe, in Lapland, northern Sweden and Norway. He died in Saint Petersburg, today's Leningrad, about to embark on an expedition across the vast Arctic reaches of the Russian Empire. His body was returned and buried here, but no files record who sponsored the move (he had no family), or who paid for this globe-like monument, appropriate for an explorer.

DUN

So you want to buy a VCR on credit, do you?

ROBERT GRAHAM (1826-1900)

Discretion well characterized Robert Graham Dun's system of gathering and distributing credit information reliable enough to allow credit to take the place of scarce capital. By emphasizing quantifiable measures such as capital worth, cash flow and debt instead of the qualitative measures of a businessman's moral character and personal habits, Dun changed the nature of the business from credit *reporting* to credit *rating*. His first regular credit reference book rated over 20,000 businesses in the United States and Canada. It was bound in dark sheepskin, and a brass lock and key kept it confidential from the prying eyes of a subscriber's subordinates or office visitors.

DURANT

Carriage maker William C. Durant bought out inventor David Buick's motor car company in 1904, improved the manufacture of the car's axles, hired the Chevrolet brothers to drive it in highly-publicized cross-country races, and built it into America's number one automobile by 1908. In that year he incorporated General Motors and went out to buy up other makes. He could have bought out Henry Ford for $3 million, but doubtful bankers held him back. In 1918 General Motors was, nevertheless, recapitalized at one billion dollars, making it America's second billion-dollar corporation, after United States Steel (today's USX).

WILLIAM C. (1861-1947)

"A time will come," William C. Durant confidently predicted in 1908, "when half a million automobiles a year will be running on the roads of this country." At the time Durant was the world's largest manufacturer of carriages and buggies, but a banker from whom Durant sought a loan was incredulous about Durant's crazy new venture. "If that fellow has any sense," he harrumphed, "he'll keep those observations to himself."

Durant got his financing elsewhere, and went on to build General Motors Corporation, which he always called "my baby." Durant eventually overextended himself and bankers elbowed him out of control. In 1936 Durant filed for personal bankruptcy, listing liabilities of $914,000 and assets of only $250, his clothes. His unflagging energy drove him into other business ventures, however, including, at the time of his death, a drive-in restaurant, a new spark plug company and a suburban supermarket. "I haven't a dollar," he said, "but I'm happy and I'm carrying on because I can't stop. There's much more to life than money." His baby survives.

The incredulous banker who refused that early loan, George W. Perkins (1862-1920), lies here at Woodlawn too, about one hundred yards away from Durant's mausoleum. He was a partner in J. P. Morgan and Company.

Duke Ellington won nationwide attention in the 1920's through his radio broadcasts live from Harlem's "jumpin'" Cotton Club. His songs such as "Sophisticated Lady," "It Don't Mean a Thing If It Ain't Got That Swing," and "I Got It Bad and That Ain't Good" became popular hits, while his instrumentals such as "Black and Tan Fantasy" became overnight jazz classics.

EDWARD KENNEDY (1889-1974)

Duke Ellington's formal musical education was halted at age seven, when his teacher (Mrs. Clinkscales, he said) rejected him for playing off-tone chords, but if jazz is America's classical music, Duke Ellington became America's greatest classical composer. He brought distinction to jazz, not only social, taking it from Harlem clubs to the White House, Carnegie Hall, and Westminster Abbey, but, more important, musical distinction. He published over 900 compositions ranging from popular songs to symphonic and religious pieces; a substantial body of work standing comparison with any European or American modern composer.

Ellington was the only composer since Haydn to assemble his own orchestra and to use it as a compositional workshop through decades. "Ellington plays the piano," said his longtime collaborator, Billy Strayhorn, "but his real instrument is his band." Ellington recorded for almost a half-century, and thank Heaven

for that, because his scores couldn't be played quite the same by any other group! The effects of harmony and timbre which he achieved in performance could not be captured by notation, although Paul Whiteman, Ferde Grofe and others spent night after night at the Cotton Club trying. Even master colorists such as Debussy, Delius and Ravel, with whom the Duke is often compared, are left behind.

The honors and awards which he won are too numerous to list, but culminate in the Presidential Medal of Freedom, America's highest civilian award. He received that in 1969 at a birthday party at the White House, where his father had served as a butler.

The Duke's funeral overcrowded the Cathedral of Saint John the Divine, the world's largest. Ella Fitzgerald sang his song "Solitude" and the old New Orleans funeral hymn "Just a Closer Walk with Thee," and then the Duke was brought to Woodlawn and laid to rest beside his parents.

FARRAGUT

Mobile Bay provided the last refuge for Confederate blockade runners during the Civil War, protected by its mines, forts and ships. Farragut eliminated that refuge with his bold run into the Bay on August 5, 1864, and his defeat of the Confederate flotilla there. The city itself did not surrender until April 1865. (*Harper's Weekly*, September 3, 1864.)

ADMIRAL DAVID GLASGOW (1801-1870)

Admiral David Farragut, America's first officer to hold that rank, lies beneath this broken draped mast, symbol of a hero's life cut short. Around the base of the mast are flags, swords and other insignia of naval warfare, and the arms of the United States. Farragut was braced high up on a mast for a good view of the Battle of Mobile Bay when he roared his famous command, "Damn the torpedoes! Full speed ahead!" Admiral Farragut descended from Spanish grandees who had officered the Spanish Armada in 1588 and his own father, Jorge Ferragut (sic), had volunteered and served heroically in the American War of Independence.

The Admiral was laid to rest here after a funeral procession up Broadway which was followed by President U.S. Grant and his entire Cabinet.

The obelisk visible behind Farragut's column marks the grave
of his good friend, Commodore Henry Eagle (1801-1882), whose
1861 attack on Sewell's Point, outside Norfolk, was the Union's first
naval offensive in the Civil War.

FITCH

CLYDE (1865-1909)

Clyde Fitch was not only America's most popular turn-of-the-century playwright, with five hits at one time running on Broadway simultaneously, but also the first American playwright to win international acclaim. His 36 original plays, 21 adaptations, and 5 dramatizations of novels introduced American subjects and American manners to the stage. They mark, according to Van Wyck Brooks, "the beginning of an American drama of interest and importance."

Fitch's popular drawing-room comedies won him the title "the American Congreve," but his total output was extraordinarily diverse. Historical dramas include "Nathan Hale" (1898), "Barbara Frietchie" (1899, set to music by Sigmund Romberg as "My Maryland" in 1927), and "Major Andre" (1903), a sympathetic portrayal of the British officer who negotiated Benedict Arnold's betrayal of West Point. Psychological dramas include "The Girl with the Green Eyes" (1902), which has been called "the best study of jealousy since 'Othello,'" and "The Truth" (1907), which was translated and performed internationally. Greta Garbo starred in a 1931 screen version of Fitch's "Sapho" (1900), which was retitled "Inspiration."

Playwright Clyde Fitch's swag-draped sarcaphogus, protected by a Tuscan canopy, was designed by Richard and Joseph Hunt, the sons of Richard Morris Hunt. It is patterned after the tomb of a Russian princess in Paris' Pére Lachaise Cemetery. The playwright died at the age of 45, largely from overwork, and mourners overcrowded the funeral ceremony at Fifth Avenue's Episcopalian Church of the Ascension.

GARVAN

When President Harding demanded the return to the government of German chemical patents, Garvan refused to cooperate, although, seen in the center here, he did present documents and records to a grand jury. Garvan took the offensive, suggesting that "the sudden and peculiar attitude of the President" may have, corruptly, been instigated by Germans. Garvan's insinuations won credence when a jury sent Garvan's successor as Alien Property Custodian to prison for accepting a bribe for returning other German property seized during the War! Two juries hung on the question of sending Harding's own Attorney General to prison too.

FRANCIS P. (1875-1937)

Francis P. Garvan, who was appointed Alien Property Custodian by President Wilson during World War I, sold to himself, as President of the Chemical Foundation, Inc., confiscated German patents potentially worth millions of dollars. Needless to say, this looked suspicious to many people, and when Wilson's successor, President Harding, ordered the patents' return to the government in 1922, many Republicans hoped a scandal would be uncovered which would besmirch the Wilson Administration. After months of testimony in a federal courtroom, however, Garvan's actions and integrity were upheld absolutely. "The defendant," ruled the judge, "has kept the faith."

By transferring German chemical patents to a Foundation which then licensed their use to Americans, Garvan helped establish the modern American chemical industry. Foundation income subsidized the American Chemical Society, the National

Research Council, chemical laboratories at leading universities, and the publication *Chemical Abstracts*. Garvan inaugurated and personally funded both the American Chemical Society's annual school essay contest and the Garvan Prize for Women in chemistry, both of which are still awarded today.

Garvan's funeral was held at Saint Patrick's Cathedral, and his body was brought to rest in this magnificent mausoleum designed by John Russell Pope. The beautiful frieze of mourners was created by Edward Sanford, Jr., who also sculpted the two colossal groups at the Bronx County Courthouse and most of the decorative sculpture in California's State Capitol in Sacramento. From the mausoleum's steps you can sometimes hear the chapel bells at Fordham University, where Garvan served as Dean of Law from 1919 to 1923.

DUNNE

FINLEY PETER (1867-1936)

The Garvan mausoleum also contains the remains of Garvan's good friend, Finley Peter Dunne, whose fictional saloonkeeper "Martin Dooley" entertained Americans with his incisive but humorous commentary on social and political affairs. ("Politics ain't beanbag.") Dooley's monologues explained to a customer, "Hennessey," the meaning of the current affairs reported elsewhere in the newspaper. ("The modern idea of politics is: snub the people, buy the people, and jaw the people.") Dooley won his greatest fame with his gibes at the Spanish-American War and America's turn-of-the-century imperialist forays ("The enthusiasm of this country always makes me think of a bonfire on an icefloe. It burns bright so long as you feed it, but it don't take hold, somehow, on the ice."), but many of his comments are as fresh today as when written. ("A fanatic is a man who does what he thinks the Lord would do if He knew the facts in the case.") Who today doubts that "The Supreme Court follows the election returns?" and in 1905 Dunne wrote, "A subject race is really funny only when it's subject. About three years ago I stopped laughing at Japanese jokes."

Francis Garvan (one of whose sons was named Peter Dunne Garvan) arranged Dunne's funeral, which was held at Saint Patrick's Cathedral, and Dunne was interred here.

JOHN W. (1855-1911)

John "Bet-a-Million" Gates made his first fortune by introducing barbed wire into Texas—"light as air, stronger than whiskey, and cheaper than dirt," he boasted. He eventually sold his wire company to United States Steel and went on to build a second fortune by founding Texaco. He'd probably be happy to know that a Texaco station stands just outside Woodlawn's gates.

CHARLES (1876-1913)

John's son, Charlie, earned his nickname "Spend-a-Million" by testing his own proposition that "Speed is life." He died of apoplexy at the age of 37 after a drinking bout with his pal, Buffalo Bill.

The Gates mausoleum reproduces a classical Greek temple in the Doric style, and the grieving figure on the door was designed by sculptor Robert Aitken, who also designed the west portal of the Supreme Court building in Washington, D.C. Movie fans may remember the mausoleum from Sergio Leone's "Once Upon a Time in America." Star Robert DeNiro visited this mausoleum as supposedly that of a childhood friend.

Gould, "The sins of Erie lie buried here." Justice, "I am not that blind, Mr. Gould."

In 1872, Jay Gould tried to blame his late partner, Jim Fisk, for the mismanagement and looting of the Erie Railroad, but this popular Thomas Nast cartoon insisted that Justice was not blind to Gould's guilt in the affair. (*Harper's Weekly*, February 24, 1872.)

JAY (1836-1892)

Financier Jay Gould was so bold and so crafty that during his lifetime he was called "the Mephistopheles of Wall Street, the most hated man in America," and when he died the *New York Times* curtly noted "Jay Gould's Career Ended." The *London Times,* however, a more detached observer, trumpeted, "All honor to the greatest money maker of any age or clime. He was less a man than a machine for churning wealth. Napoleon's combinations were never vaster. . . . It will be impossible to explain one phase of civilization without a frequent mention of his name." In fact the jury's still out on whether he was more wicked or just smarter than jealous rivals.

Gould's hilltop mausoleum is a miniature Ionic temple, designed by architect H. Q. French of New York. The enormous weeping beech (*Fagus sylvatica* 'Pendula') which almost threatens to engulf it was designated one of the "113 Great Trees of New York City" in 1985.

George first discovered and mapped Grinnell Glacier in Montana in 1885, and he led the fight to set aside the land for what became our Glacier National Park. George had also been the first to map the Black Hills of South Dakota in 1874 (with his pal George Custer, whom Grinnell later luckily declined to accompany to the Little Big Horn in 1876), and Wyoming's Yellowstone Valley in 1875. He later served for many years as president of the National Parks Association.

GEORGE (1849-1938)

George Grinnell, founder of the first Audubon Society (1886), longtime owner-editor of *Forest and Stream* magazine, and author of many classic books on wildlife, as well as on American Indian life and lore, launched the American conservation movement.

Grinnell was a patrician Easterner by birth, but his first trip out West, as part of an 1870 fossil-hunting expedition, impressed him with Nature's vulnerability. The expedition found fossils of over 100 extinct vertebrate species, providing enough evidence of Darwin's theory of evolution to astonish Darwin himself. Grinnell later spearheaded efforts to protect the buffalo, which shrank in numbers from the millions Grinnell saw in 1870 to only a few hundred animals left by 1894. Grinnell befriended the Indians, who were in almost as much danger of being wiped out as the buffalo were, and he was made an honorary member of several tribes. His books *Pawnee Hero Stories* (1889), *The Story of the Indian* (1895), and *The Cheyenne Indians* (1923) won him recognition as one of America's greatest anthropologists.

By calling attention to the degradation and depletion of our natural resources and beauty, he woke Americans to an appreciation of our precious natural heritage and inspired us to save it.

This cartoon assails the one occasion on which Senator Simon Guggenheim, who represented Colorado from 1907 to 1913, maneuvered in favor of family financial interests. In 1910, during the Taft presidency, the Guggenheims and J. P. Morgan sought to exploit Alaska's mineral resources. The "Guggenmorgan Syndicate" is recognizably Simon. The syndicate was opposed, however, by the popular Director of the Forest Service, Gifford Pinchot, and by former President Teddy Roosevelt, who had appointed Pinchot. When Senator Guggenheim attacked Pinchot in the Senate, Roosevelt broke with President Taft, splitting the Republican Party, and opening the way for the election of Democrat Woodrow Wilson in 1912.

SIMON (1867-1941) and
OLGA HIRSCH (1877-1970)

Simon Guggenheim and his wife, Olga, donated millions of dollars to educational institutions in Colorado, ("Have a school, on me," he used to say genially), but they put their giving on a permanent and institutional basis when their young son, John Simon (1905-1922) died. They set up the John Simon Guggenheim Memorial Foundation in order "to promote the advancement and diffusion of knowledge and understanding and the appreciation of beauty" adding to "the educational, literary, artistic and scientific power of this country . . . under the freest possible conditions." The 15,000 "Guggenheim Fellows" up to 1988 have gathered 54 Nobel Prizes, 138 Pulitzer Prizes, and countless other awards and honors. No other public or private program has so generously fostered individual scientific or artistic creativity on such a scale.

The Guggenheim family columbarium (a repository for ashes) is decorated in the Gothic style. The Chi Rho, XP, on the shield above the door is a contraction of the name Christ in Greek, and it is among the oldest of Christian symbols.

At Handy's funeral, Reverend Adam Clayton Powell, Jr. said, "Gabriel now has an understudy—a side man. And when the last trumpet shall sound I am sure that W. C. Handy will be there." An estimated 150,000 people lined the route of the funeral procession to Woodlawn.

WILLIAM C. (1873-1958)

W.C. Handy was "The Father of the Blues," and his headstone records the opening notes of his "Saint Louis Blues," arguably the most popular song in American history. William's father, a freed slave who had become a Methodist minister, strongly disapproved of secular music, but W.C. traveled throughout the South with a minstrel show band, collecting and absorbing all the traditional black musical forms. He wrote them down and got them published, paving the way for public acceptance and development of black music other than spirituals. Handy's "Memphis Blues" is often called the first piece of composed jazz. He came to New York in 1918, joined in music publishing and recording ventures, and later authored several books on music. In 1928 he could lecture at Carnegie Hall on the origins and development of Afro-American music, but he was still banned from "Whites Only" Harlem clubs which featured his own compositions.

HARKNESS

In Egypt's "Valley of the Kings" Edward Harkness listens attentively as archeologist Albert Lythgoe explains a fine point of Egyptian history. Harkness donations of Egyptian antiquities to the Metropolitan Museum highlight its collection, one of the world's finest.

EDWARD (1874-1940)

In 1867, Cleveland capitalist Stephen V. Harkness invested $75,000 in John D. Rockefeller's fledgling Standard Oil Company, and the Harkness fortune burgeoned with the Rockefellers'. What's interesting about the Harknesses, however, is not how they made their money, but how assiduously they gave it away. Stephen's son, Edward, gave away more money of his own than any other man in history, writing out personal checks for millions of dollars for medical schools and hospitals (including New York's Columbia-Presbyterian and Baltimore's Johns Hopkins), university facilities across America, entire art collections for museums and countless charities.

Edward devoted most of his life to guiding the Commonwealth Fund, chartered by his mother in 1918 rather vaguely "to do something for mankind." The Fund built a distinguished record of analyzing Americans' health care needs and designing pilot projects for delivering health care. The Fund pioneered clinical services in child psychology, child pyschiatry and psychiatric social work; it built pediatric clinics across the country, and eventually entire hospitals where needed in many rural areas. Public agencies have gradually assumed responsibility for several of these programs. Today the Commonwealth Fund is investigating the needs of America's elderly, particularly those living alone. What services can be provided to them in their homes to help them maintain their independence and integrity?

Edward Harkness commissioned this miniature chapel mausoleum from architect James Gamble Rogers, who also designed the several buildings Harkness gave to Yale University. Each Christmas the teakwood gate you see here is decorated with a wreath sent from the Commonwealth Fund.

Victor Herbert, his wife Therese Foerster Herbert (1861-1927), and their daughter Ella vacationed at Lake Placid in 1908. Herbert had been born in Ireland, but educated in Germany, and Therese Foerster had been the leading soprano of the Stuttgart Court Opera when Victor was the principal cellist there. They fell in love, married in 1886, and shortly thereafter came to New York to work together at the Metropolitan Opera. Mrs. Herbert undoubtedly deserves some credit for the extraordinary sensitivity to singers' requirements and capabilities that characterizes Victor's operettas.

VICTOR (1859-1924)

Victor Herbert's operettas demonstrate an inexhaustible gift for beautiful melodies, a mastery of orchestration, a superlative understanding of what can be expected of the human voice, and a keen sense of theatrical appropriateness. "The Fortune Teller," "Babes in Toyland," "Mademoiselle Modiste," "The Red Mill," "Naughty Marietta," and others of the forty operettas he wrote will always be in performance somewhere, and individual songs ("Gypsy Love Song," "Ah, Sweet Mystery of Life," "The Time and the Place and the Girl" . . . pick your own favorites) will never lack appreciation.

Herbert's fame as a composer overshadows his other contributions to music in America as a cello soloist, a conductor and a leader of the artistic community. His testimony helped fashion American musical copyright law and, already a rich man himself, he helped others insure rewards from their work when he helped found The American Society of Composers, Authors and Publishers (ASCAP), which protects artists' rights.

Herbert is one of the few artists honored with a portrait bust in Central Park, unveiled in 1927.

Hughes married Antoinette Carter (1864-1945), the daughter of a senior partner in the New York City law firm he joined as a young man, and the contentment of their life together was a source of great strength to Mr. Hughes through his long and active life. Is she reading here, or catching forty winks?

CHARLES EVANS (1862-1948)

Charles Evans Hughes was a reserved, austere man—"the bearded iceberg," Teddy Roosevelt called him—and yet his whole life was a series of astonishing surprises. In 1905 Hughes, a conservative Republican lawyer, probed and thoroughly exposed corruption in two major New York industries: natural gas utilities and life insurance. He went on to serve as a progressive state governor and then as a United States Supreme Court Justice. In 1916 he stepped down from the Supreme Court in order to run for President, the only man ever to do so, and he lost by just a hair's breadth. In 1921, as President Harding's Secretary of State, Hughes proposed significant world disarmament, listing before a breathless international audience the battleships the United States was actually willing to scrap. In 1930, he was returned to the Supreme Court (another act unprecedented or imitated in American history), this time as Chief Justice. He ran afoul of President Franklin Roosevelt when the Court overturned the National Industrial Recovery Act and the Agricultural Adjustment Act, but later the Hughes court approved equally progressive New Deal legislation. Hughes retired from the bench in 1941, generally regarded as one of our greatest Chief Justices.

The Reverend Harry Emerson Fosdick officiated at Hughes' funeral services at Riverside Church and also at simple graveside services here at Woodlawn, while flags flew at half-staff across America. Hughes' unpretentious plot with simple ledger stones well reflects the man's nature, and his descent from Baptist ministers.

HUNTINGTON

COLLIS P. (1821-1900)

Collis P. Huntington was, to his own immense satisfaction, the only man ever to be able to ride from coast to coast on his own railroad tracks. From Newport News, Virginia, a city which he had founded and where he built the world's largest shipyards, he could ride on his Chesapeake and Ohio Railroad to the city of Huntington, West Virginia, named for him, and on across to the west coast on his Southern Pacific Railroad.

Collis had been born in Upstate New York (Oneonta—later the name of his private railroad car), but had gone out to California during the gold rush. There he and his partners Mark Hopkins, Charles Crocker and Leland Stanford ("The Big Four") built many businesses, including the Central Pacific Railroad, which met Sidney Dillon's Union Pacific to form the first transcontinental line in 1869. The Big Four rose to virtual rule of California, although they later split up bitterly.

ARCHER (1870-1955)

Collis was eventually joined here by his son, philanthropist Archer Huntington, who built and endowed art museums and libraries across America and in Spain, and his daughter-in-law, sculptor Anna Hyatt Huntington.

ANNA HYATT (1876-1973)

Anna Hyatt Huntington, Collis' daughter-in-law, won worldwide renown for her animal sculptures and equestrian portraits. Here, at the age of 71 (she worked into her 90's), she works on her monument to the fictional Don Quixote. This statue stands in Brookgreen Sculpture Gardens and Park, Anna and her husband Archer's gift to the State of South Carolina; a bas-relief of the figure can be seen in the outdoor terraces of New York's Hispanic Society Museum, one of the Huntingtons' gifts to New York City. Anna's equestrian portrait of Cuban liberator José Marti towers over New York's Central Park at the head of the Avenue of the Americas. From the steps of the Huntington mausoleum you can almost see the Bronx Zoo, where the young Anna had learned to model animal figures.

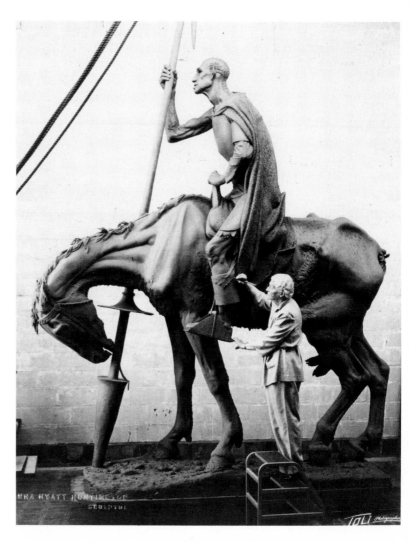

Huntington was American's largest landowner, and he traveled among many homes and estates scattered across the country, but he chose to be buried here at Woodlawn. Architect Robert Caterson designed this enormous granite and marble mausoleum, which measures 42 feet by 28 feet by 24 feet high. It took five years to build. Caterson modeled the grand staircase after one in New York's Pennsylvania Railroad Station.

JOHN (1844-1896)

Young Confederate veteran John Inman returned to his family's Tennessee plantation only to find the plantation in ruins and his family impoverished. He came north and dedicated himself first to amassing a personal fortune in the New York Cotton Exchange and in real estate, and secondly to funneling over $100 million of Yankee investment into the defeated South for reconstruction and industrialization.

When John came north, his brother Samuel went to Atlanta where Samuel soon emerged as that city's "first citizen." The brothers coordinated their investments in cotton trading, then in developing the Southern iron and steel industry, and then in Southern railroads. Inman-controlled lines eventually formed the giant Southern Railway System. John and Samuel served together as directors of many corporations throughout the South, and of the several great exhibitions which boosted Atlanta during the 1880's. An 1889 history of Atlanta writes of the family's "credit and prestige that is simply without limit." The full history of this extraordinary family has yet to be written.

John Inman always referred to himself as a Southerner, and upon his death the *Atlanta Constitution* would praise "this warm friend of the South," but the *New York Times* would simultaneously claim that "New York has adopted no son that has brought her more honor."

JULLIARD

The student Juilliard Orchestra has won acclaim on its travels around the world, and it offers regular free concerts at its New York City home.

AUGUSTUS D. (1836-1919)

Itzhak Perlman and Tito Puente, Leontyne Price and Marvin Hamlisch, Henry Mancini and Barry Manilow, Van Cliburn, Phillip Glass and Patti Lupone are just a few graduates of the Juilliard School in New York City, the surprise legacy of industrialist Augustus D. Juilliard.

Juilliard was born at sea during his parents' immigration from Burgundy. He was raised in Ohio and came to New York only after the Civil War, and here he made his fortune in the textile business. He actively supported the musical life of New York City, serving as president of the Metropolitan Opera at the time of his death, but no one was expecting the incredible windfall for musical education which he left in his will. In fact, the *New York Times* reported his death in April 1919 on page fifteen, but the news of his astounding bequest made page one six weeks later.

Juilliard's will set aside millions of dollars to establish a

musical foundation "to aid worthy students of music," "to arrange for and to give . . . musical entertainments, concerts and recitals," and "to aid . . . the Metropolitan Opera." As the *Times* editorialized, "No benefactor for music of such scope and magnitude has ever before been known."

The Foundation immediately assumed a leading role in musical education. At first the Foundation aided the pre-existing Institute of Musical Art, but then in 1924 the Foundation founded the Juilliard Graduate School, and eventually these two merged into today's Juilliard School. Juilliard graduates enrich the performing arts in cities and towns across the United States.

HELEN COSSITT (1847-1916)

Mrs. Juilliard, born Helen Cossitt, was herself a noted philanthropist; Colorado College was among the principal recipients of her generosity. She predeceased her husband, and was brought to rest in this enormous Ionic-style mausoleum.

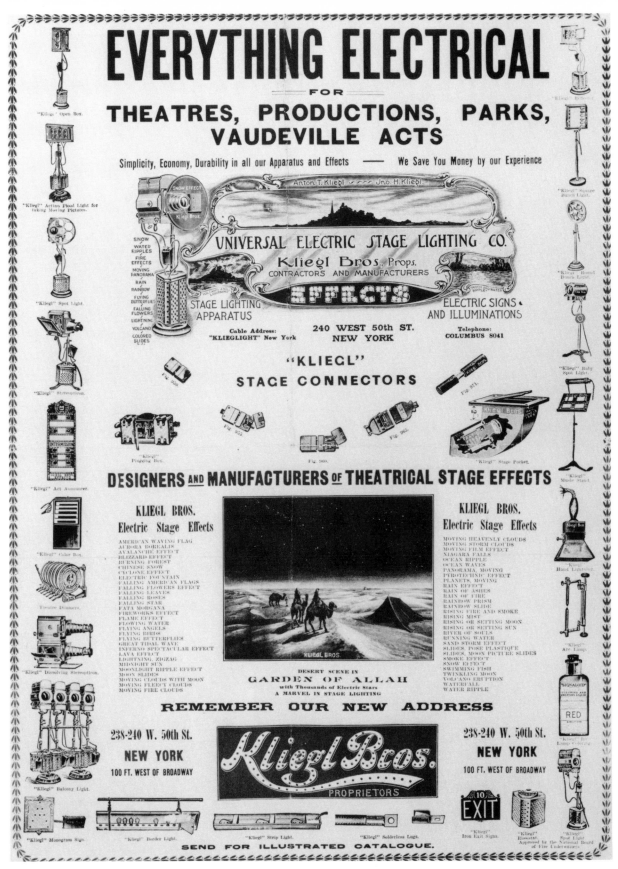

This Kliegl Brothers ad shows the variety of stage lighting devices and stage effects which had won the brothers fame already by 1911. No wonder that these advertised avalanches and blizzards, volcanoes and waterfalls thrilled audiences here and abroad! Notice too the powerful theatre dimmers; theatre electricians had previously plunged the theatre into sudden darkness at the beginning of a performance by pulling the main switch, a practice understandably annoying to the audience.

ANTON T. (1874-1927)

Thomas Edison himself praised the Kliegl brothers' continuing invention of brighter and more efficient light bulbs and lighting devices. Their stunning and innovative scenic effects on the stages of New York's theatres, at the Metropolitan Opera House, and even outdoors at spectacular public pageants were known worldwide.

And so, when the fledgling movie industry needed a new and brighter type of light than any lights yet invented for indoor filming, it turned to the Kliegls for help. About 1908 the brothers answered with their Klieglight, an intense carbon arc which provided an even, non-flickering light of uniform distribution. The Klieglight liberated moviemakers from daylight, allowing directors to film outdoor scenes in the studios and even to take cameras into theatres, factories, mines and other difficult locations. When Anton Kliegl, the founder of the family company, died in 1927, Al Jolson was just starring in the first "talkie," "The Jazz Singer," and the movie industry was about to take off.

Anton Kliegl died while on a visit to Bad Kissingen, Germany, where he had been born. Obituaries noted that he died poor, having made a fortune, but having given generously to charities through his lifetime.

KREISLER

FRITZ (1875-1962)

Fritz Kreisler began to play the violin at the age of four. He first performed publicly at nine, and he stopped taking instruction at the age of twelve because there was nothing more anyone could teach him. For the next three-quarters of a century his artistry thrilled audiences, and his own compositions are standards in the violin repertoire.

Fritz Kreisler's playing displayed not only technical brilliance, but intellectual substance and a unique sweetness of tone. Fellow violinst Joseph Szigeti would write, "If one translated Kreisler's playing style into the terms of prose style one could say: Kreisler's is the antithesis of 'purple prose.'"

Kreisler was one of the first musicians ever to record ("Old Folks at Home" in 1902) and during World War II he regularly performed over the air. When he retired in 1950 he gave to the Library of Congress a collection of precious musical manuscripts and also his favorite violin, a 1737 Joseph Guarnerius, which is arguably the finest instrument ever made.

Austrian-born violinist Fritz Kreisler married Harriet Lies in 1902, and eventually became an American citizen himself. His good friend, Bishop Fulton J. Sheen, presided at his funeral. Surely Kreisler would be met in Heaven, said the Bishop, by an angelic host singing Vieuxtemps' "Fantasie Caprice," the piece which Kreisler had played at his American debut at the age of thirteen in 1888.

Walt Kuhn's own painting is best remembered for his sympathetic portraits of circus performers and clowns. They continue an artistic tradition from Tiepolo to Toulouse-Lautrec, a tradition in which human dignity surmounts the insolence of circumstance. As a young man, Kuhn himself had worked his way across America as a stunt bicycle rider at county fairs, and portraits such as this melancholy miss, whose steadfast gaze belies the gaiety of her costume, earned Kuhn his sobriquet "the Rembrandt of show business."

WALT (1877-1944)

Artist Walt Kuhn helped put together the 1913 International Exhibition of Modern Art in a New York City armory. The show marked, Kuhn wrote, "the starting point of the new spirit in art as far as America is concerned." Works by the impressionists Renoir and Monet, the post-impressionists Cezanne and Van Gogh, and the cubists Picasso and Braque exploded like a bombshell on the American consciousness. "Pathological, hideous!" shrilled the *New York Times*, but former President Teddy Roosevelt, escorted through the exhibition by Kuhn, conceded that "there was not a touch of simpering, self-satisfied conventionality."

LaGUARDIA

FIORELLO (1882-1947)

Fiorello LaGuardia brought compassion for the underdog through a lifetime of public service as a self-described "insurgent." A friend put it another way: "The Christian concept of Heaven was very real to him, except that he believed it was achievable on earth and, if he only hurried, possible in his lifetime."

LaGuardia was born in New York City in 1882, only two years after his parents had arrived from Italy. Much was later to be made of his mixed religious background; his father was a lapsed Catholic and his mother Jewish—a cousin of Italy's first Jewish Minister. Fiorello was raised Episcopalian. He once silenced a political opponent who accused him of anti-semitism by challenging him to debate the point—in Yiddish.

Fiorello worked his way through law school as a translator on Ellis Island, and then he won election to Congress as a Republican in 1917. He almost immediately took a leave of absence to fight in World War I, and during the war he rose to the rank of Major in the Air Force. His enthusiasm for aviation is appropriately commemmorated by New York's LaGuardia Airport. Also during the war, LaGuardia, acting on personal instructions from President Wilson, stumped Italy to rally support for the war effort and to convince our ally of America's commitment. From 1923 to 1933 La Guardia returned to Congress, where he fought for legislation to regulate child labor, natural resources, and securities trading. In those years, however, his liberal agenda met little success, although he and Nebraska Senator George Norris did co-sponsor the 1932 Anti-Injunction Act, often called "the Magna Carta of organized labor."

Progressive Republican LaGuardia was, ironically, swept out of office by Franklin Roosevelt's coattails in 1932, but FDR, in a gracious gesture, chose the lame duck LaGuardia to introduce his own legislative package in the spring of 1933.

From 1934 through 1945 La Guardia served as the mayor of New York City on a fusion ticket. "There is no Democratic or Republican way to pick up garbage," he insisted. He made New York an urban showcase in slum clearance, public housing, health care and parks. His frantic activity invited caricature, but never ridicule.

Mayor La Guardia refused to run for re-election in 1945, and no one could help but notice that he was an old man at 63 when he left City Hall. In 1946 he took up the directorship of the United Nations Relief and Rehabilitation Administration, but he was tired. He died in 1947.

Mayor La Guardia was laid to rest in this modest and peaceful plot on September 20, 1947. His simple epitaph, "Statesman, Humanitarian," well epitomizes his gentle character. The tablet incorporates his name, "Little Flower."

MIRIAM (1836-1914)

When Frank Leslie died, his wife, Miriam Leslie, legally changed her name to Frank and carried on the business. A one-time stage protegee of Lola Montez, Miriam had retired from the stage and found work capably editing *Frank Leslie's Ladies' Journal* before marrying the boss in 1874. Upon inheriting the business she enforced economies to get the company back on its feet, and reigned as America's acknowledged "Empress of Journalism." She remarried in 1881, this time Oscar Wilde's older brother, William. He was known as something of a scalawag and, since the best man's name happened to be Wilder, the three before the altar were dubbed "Wilde, Wilder and Wildest." Miriam divorced William after two years.

When she died in 1914 her will almost pushed World War I off the front page. She left some $2 million to "my friend Mrs. Carrie Chapman Catt . . . to apply the whole thereof to the further-ance of the cause of woman's suffrage." Miriam's legacy financed Mrs. Catt's last victorious campaigns.

FRANK (1821-1880)

Frank Leslie learned the trade of engraver and printer at the *Illustrated London News* before migrating to the United States in 1848. Here he launched *Frank Leslie's Illustrated Newspaper*, which pioneered the format in America. Instead of using pictures only to support the text, his publications used only enough text ("mental pabulum," he called it) to describe the illustrations. Frank, himself, invented a method of dividing large pictures into several small squares for rapid execution by separate engravers, then to be reassembled and printed. This put his papers first in circulation with vivid illustrations of news events, and it proved a profitable advantage during the Civil War. Wherever soldiers went, Leslie's illustrators followed. Frank branched out to build an empire of sixteen regular publications—"market segmentation" long before the phrase was coined on Madison Avenue—boasting an aggregate circulation of 500,000 Americans per week. The depression of 1877 brought down his empire, but he was emerging from receivership when he died.

Frank and Miriam Leslie lie before this impressive monument, on the back of which we read: "In Memory of Frank Leslie. . . . The pioneer and founder of illustrated journalism in America. . . . His aim was to popularize art and make it a common helper of men. . . . He never caused any other grief than his death."

Illustrator J.C. Leyendecker created the Arrow Collar Man, a square-jawed elegant and aloof image of the American male that became an advertising icon, a heart-throb to the Flapper Era. Leyendecker's creation received more letters, gifts, proposals of marriage and notes threatening suicide if refused than even Rudolph Valentino did.

J.C. (1874-1951)

J. C. Leyendecker was a master of narrative illustration, as his 322 covers for the *Saturday Evening Post* attest, and his first published pictures were, in fact, a series of sixty illustrations for an edition of the *Bible* etched when Joe was only fifteen. It was his poster art, however, images which convey a style or stylishness without telling a story, that are probably most remembered today. The Arrow Collar Man, introduced in 1905, was a triumph. It created a wholly new image of civilized perfection, and the "character" even starred in a 1923 Broadway musical "Helen of Troy, New York" (where the collars were made).

Leyendecker himself lived the image of elegant hauteur which he created for his clients including Arrow, Kuppenheimer and Hart, Schafner & Marx Suits. Norman Rockwell, a friend of both Joe and Joe's brother, Frank, who was also an illustrator, painted a word picture of the Leyendecker brothers. "They were quite short and walked in step, with real military precision, the tips of their canes and their black and white saddle shoes hitting the pavement at precisely the same instant. They wore white flannels, double breasted blue blazers with shiny brass buttons, and stiff straw hats . . . . they were both very handsome — dark complexioned with high cheekbones and straight, delicately molded noses. Like Spaniards. And trim, well-built."

Frank died at only 47 in 1924, but he left behind a body of narrative work noted for its sensitivity and feeling. Joe joined him here in the family plot in 1951.

Photographer George Platt Lynes recorded Jerome Robbins and Maria Tallchief dancing George Balanchine's "The Prodigal Son" for the New York City Ballet in 1950. "George Lynes' pictures," wrote Balanchine, "will contain all that will be remembered of my own repertory in a hundred years. Movement will be lost, but an expert echo, however remote, will still be ringing in the photographs."

GEORGE PLATT (1907-1955)

George Platt Lynes' photographs are today collected and displayed in art museums, and celebrated and reproduced in lavish new books. His appreciation as a major American artist is widening.

George first went to Paris as a brilliant and restless teenager in 1926, and there he was soon drawn into the expatriate American literary and artistic circle around Gertrude Stein. Lynes picked up a camera and began a series of photographic portraits of his new friends, including writers Andre Gide, Jean Cocteau, Ernest Hemingway and artist Marsden Hartley. George joined Man Ray in exploring ways in which the camera could extend the possibilities of the new art movement, surrealism, with its startling images of surprisingly juxtaposed objects, as in dreams. An artful double exposure, for instance, can "show us things we could never see."

As George's surrealist experiments won international attention, he continued with his celebrity portraiture and also demonstrated a gift for fashion photography. By the end of the 1930's he was America's number one fashion and portrait photographer. Just before his death he destroyed the negatives of all of his fashion photographs, preferring to be remembered only by his surrealistic works, his portraits, and his ballet photographs. On these works alone, his reputation is secure.

MASTERSON

WILLIAM "BAT" (1853-1921)

They say lawman Bat Masterson shot his way into Heaven—not by storming the Pearly Gates, but by sending enough bad men to "the other place" so that decent people could live in peace. As buffalo hunter, army scout, Sheriff of Dodge City, Kansas, Marshal of Trinidad, Colorado, and later, by appointment of President Teddy Roosevelt, a deputy federal Marshal, Bat personified the legendary Wild West. *The Dodge City Times* described him in 1877: "Bat is a well-known young man of nerve and coolness. . . . He knows just how to gather in the sinners and will never shrink from danger."

Bat Masterson doesn't lie on Boot Hill, but here in the Bronx. Bat hung up his guns and ended his days as a popular sports columnist. He had long encouraged sport boxing, and even officiated at the 1897 bout at which Bob Fitzsimmons took the world heavyweight title from James J. "Gentleman Jim" Corbett. Bat's friend, Jack Dempsey, later used to kid him that Bat didn't really know much about boxing, having lost a bundle by betting on Jess Willard against Dempsey in the 1919 title bout.

Bat died suddenly while working at his desk at the *New York Morning Telegraph,* and in his typewriter was the ironic opening for his next day's column, which will have to stand as Bat's last words, "We all get the same amount of ice. The rich get it in the summertime, and the poor get it in winter."

Bat's pals, boxing promoter Tex Rickard and writer Damon Runyon saw Bat to rest here at Woodlawn. Bat's friend, Alfred Henry Lewis (1859-1914), whose popular Western tales immortalized Bat, rests just a few yards away. (Please note date on tombstone, 1854, is incorrect.)

HERMAN (1819-1891)

Legend has it that author Herman Melville designed his own gravestone, a blank scroll, as a bitter comment on the impermanence of his own written achievement. Reviewers had greeted *Moby Dick* with derision. "Mad as a March hare; gibbering, screaming, like an incurable Bedlamite, reckless of keeper or straight-jacket," wrote one. Why, asked readers, had the writer of the popular South Seas adventures *Typee*, *Omoo*, and *Mardi* written this baffling saga? Today those earlier adventure tales continue to win new readers, but *Moby Dick* has risen to general regard as one of the greatest of all American novels.

Herman had gone to sea at nineteen in order to escape the humiliation of his once-aristocratic family's descent into genteel poverty. A voyage on a whaling ship, he wrote, was "my Yale College and my Harvard." His true-life experiences at sea provided the inspiration for his first popular novels; he jumped ship in the South Pacific, was captured by cannibals, escaped, worked on island plantations and then signed aboard a Navy frigate in Hawaii in order to get back to the United States. Melville's first books celebrated South Seas primitive life at the expense of Western civilization ("snivelization"), giving his readers exotic romances, erotic dreams of a Polynesia of coral reefs and coconuts.

The appearance of *Moby Dick*, however, in 1851, marked the beginning of Melville's decline in popularity. Readers found the novel too dense, too obscure, and Melville sank into a depresson so deep that his wife and friends feared for his sanity. By 1852, Melville's heyday as a popular author was already over; he was 32.

Herman spent the rest of his life as an obscure customs inspector on Manhattan's Gansevoort Street piers named, ironically, for his grandfather, a Revolutionary War hero. He once visited the elegant Gansevoort Hotel, and when he found that the clerks could not tell him who Gansevoort had been, he went home "and moralized upon the instability of human glory and the evanescence of—many other things."

Today we have rediscovered Melville, and we read him not only as an outstanding writer of the sea and a great stylist, but also as a shrewd social critic and philosopher. Critics argue endlessly over allegorical meanings in *Moby Dick*, but Somerset Maugham reminded us that "*Moby Dick* may be read, and read with passionate interest, without a thought of what allegorical significance it may or may not have."

Elizabeth Shaw Melville (1822-1906) was the daughter of Massachusetts Supreme Court Chief Justice Lemuel Shaw, whose written opinions set many American legal precedents. He had been a good friend of Herman's father.

Here at Melville's grave in 1932, at midnight, Dr. John Condon, the intermediary in the Lidbergh kidnapping case, met with the man later suspected to have been Bruno Hauptmann, in a futile effort to recover the kidnapped child.

No Rest for the Wicked—Sentenced to More Hard Labor.

This Thomas Nast self-portrait appeared in *Harper's Weekly*, December 2, 1876. Nast's cartoon portraits were wonderfully accurate likenesses, and those of Jay Gould and of William Whitney in this book were immediately recognizable.

THOMAS (1840-1902)

Behind this rueful quip lies political cartoonist Thomas Nast, who originated both the donkey symbol of the Democratic Party (first used in 1870), and the Republican elephant (first used in 1874). He also gave us our popular image of Santa Claus in a series of Christmas illustrations for *Harper's Weekly* beginning in 1863.

Nast won his first illustrating job at the age of fifteen when he called on Frank Leslie and asked for work. Leslie, intending gently to discourage the boy, told him to go down to the docks and draw the crowd getting off the Hoboken ferry. Nast came back with such a fine drawing, including a few light touches which made for good popular illustration, that Leslie hired him on the spot. Nast later illustrated Civil War battles, and his political cartoons did so much to encourage the Northern spirit that President Lincoln called him "our best recruiting sergeant."

After the War, Nast launched cartoon attacks on New York City's corrupt Tweed Ring, which he dubbed the "Tammany Tiger." Tweed boasted that he didn't care what anybody wrote about him because nobody read the paper, but he did fear Nast's cartoons. When Tweed cronies offered Nast $100,000 to go to Europe "to study art," Nast declined, saying, "I shall be busy here for some time getting a bunch of thieves behind bars." Leading ring members were sent to jail in 1872.

Nast published his last illustration in 1901, the year he accepted President Teddy Roosevelt's appointment to the United States consulship in Guayaquil, Ecuador. ("I ought to make a good official," Roosevelt had told Nast. "I learned my politics from your cartoons.") Nast succumbed to yellow fever there in 1902, but only four years later was his body returned to the United States for burial here at Woodlawn.

Hideyo Noguchi's childhood home is today preserved as a museum in Inawashiro, Japan, about 120 miles north of Tokyo. Noguchi was one of the first Japanese to win world-wide recognition after Japan emerged from centuries of self-imposed isolation. "It is a citizen's duty," he wrote, "to achieve something and let the name of his country be known to the world."

Nothing in Hideyo's background favored him for world renown. His father was an alcoholic wastral who abandoned his family; his mother was a peasant so poor that one day the infant Hideyo forever crippled his left hand by crawling into the open fire pit of this peasant cottage while she worked in the fields. Noguchi refused to let his handicap discourage his studies, and his obvious genius attracted a series of distinguished patrons. Noguchi came to America in 1900, and he was one of the first scientists asked to join the prestigious Rockefeller Institute, today's Rockefeller University, when it was established in 1903.

HIDEYO (1876-1928)

This boulder marking the grave of bacteriologist Hideyo Noguchi is one of Woodlawn's most frequently visited spots. Noguchi called himself "a scientific soldier for medicine," and he discovered the causes of many diseases before he himself succumbed to yellow fever while in Africa investigating the cause of that dreaded disease. "Through devotion to science," reads the plaque, "he lived and died for humanity."

CHICAGO IN 1833.

ESTABLISHED 1865

THE Chicago Varnish Co.

MANUFACTURERS OF

"THE STANDARD" RAILWAY VARNISHES AND JAPANS

204 to 208 PINE ST, CHICAGO.

CHICAGO IN 1883.

These views of Chicago from an advertising pamphlet illustrate the years of Ogden's leadership in the city, a half century during which the population rose from about 200 in 1833 to over one-half million in 1883. The 1883 bird's eye view emphasizes the city's clearly laid out grid pattern, the industries along the Chicago River, the many types of ships in the busy harbor, and the Illinois Central Railroad on its lakefront trestle.

WILLIAM (1805-1877)

William Ogden's tomb is here at Woodlawn, but his monument is the City of Chicago, which he built and owned. His first impression of that place in 1835 however, had not been auspicious. Ogden had gone out west to investigate a relative's property speculation and, upon seeing the property, then a marshy wilderness blanketed with prairie grass and wild onions ("checagou" in Potawatomi), Ogden had written, "You have been guilty of the grossest folly."

Ogden returned to Chicago the next year to sell the property for what he could, but he ended up staying to be elected the city's first mayor when it incorporated in 1837, and, for the next forty years, there was not a single Chicago improvement or institution in which Ogden did not play a leading role. He promoted port facilities on Lake Michigan and the construction of the Chicago River Canal to link Lake Michigan to the Mississippi River. He helped spin the web of railroads which focused on Chicago and won it dominance of the North American heartland. He lead investment in local manufacturing, and it was he who loaned the young Virginian, Cyrus McCormick, the start-up capital to manufacture his reapers there, at the edge of the wheatlands. Ogden presided over the Chicago Board of Trade, the University of Chicago, the Historical Society, the Theological Seminary, the Academy of Sciences and Rush Medical College. No one lost more property in the great Chicago fire of 1871 than Ogden did, but no one was quicker to roll up his sleeves and rebuild than was Ogden, then 66 years old.

He divided his last years between Chicago and his great Bronx estate "Villa Boscobel," where he died in 1877.

The monumental statue of Lincoln in the Memorial in Washington, D.C., is probably the Piccirillis' most famous work. Daniel Chester French provided a five-foot-high clay model, and the Piccirillis carved the figure twenty-two feet high out of twenty-eight blocks of Georgia marble, supervised its loading onto eleven railroad cars, its transportation to Washington, and its construction in the Memorial in 1932. Here Getulio Piccirilli (1847-1945), on the ladder, adds final touches.

This mother and child figure, named "Fortitude," was designed by Attilio Piccirilli (1866-1945). It can be admired in marble on the Maine Monument in Manhattan, at the William Randolph Hearst collection at San Simeon in California and here in bronze on the grave of the Piccirilli family matriarch.

The six Piccirilli brothers operated a family sculpture studio in the Bronx of a sort typical in their native Carrara, Italy. Here they carved the stone sculptures and decorations for Canada's Parliament House in Winnipeg, the Boston Public Library, and the greatest private mansions, public buildings and monuments in New York City. Much of the work was of their own design, such as the portrait busts of Presidents Jefferson and Monroe in the rotunda of the Virginia State Capitol, the sculptural groups in the north pediment of the Wisconsin State Capitol, and the Maine Monument at the southwest corner of New York's Central Park. The brothers also realized, in stone, the designs of many other artists. J. Q. A. Ward, F. MacMonnies, A. Saint Gaudens, and R. I. Aitken all called on the Piccirillis to carve designs from small scale models. Statues and monuments across America which bear these other artists' names were actually carved by the Piccirillis.

PULITZER

Pulitzer abandoned his journalistic standards when he competed with W. R. Hearst to provoke the 1898 Spanish-American War, which American Secretary of State John Hay called "a splendid little war." The *real* war, observers noted, was the circulation war between Pulitzer's *World* and Hearst's *Journal*. Pulitzer introduced a cartoon "The Yellow Kid," soon copied by Hearst, which gave birth to the phrase "yellow journalism."

JOSEPH (1847-1911)

Newspaperman Joseph Pulitzer and his family lie in front of this simple classical *exedra* (bench) designed by architect Duncan Chandler. American sculptor William Ordway Partridge provided the contemplative bronze figure.

It was a Pulitzer newspaper campaign which raised the money to erect the Statue of Liberty by public subscription; each donor got his name listed in Pulitzer's *World*. Not entirely coincidentally, the campaign sold papers. Pulitzer's constant purpose was to sell more papers in order to crusade for good government. "First fill the pews," he said, "then preach."

Pulitzer left generous bequests to found America's first professional school of journalism and to establish the prestigious Pulitzer Prizes awarded annually "for the encouragement of public service, public morals, American literature, and the advancement of education."

MICHAEL (1858-1935)

Every time you make a long distance telephone call, tune your radio to a new station, or get X-rayed by your doctor, you are using one of the many practical inventions of Michael Pupin. His inventions contribute substantially to our daily life, and yet he had arrived in America at the age of fifteen, alone, speaking no English, and with only five cents in his pocket. When he wrote his autobiography in 1922 he regretted that the immigration laws then in force would have kept him out! That autobiography, *From Immigrant to Inventor*, won a Pulitzer Prize; an abridgement served nationwide as a school reader on citizenship.

In 1902, when this photograph was taken, Pupin already had a world-wide reputation, and he had just been appointed professor of the new science of electro-mechanics at Columbia University.

A bench marks the Pupin family plot at Woodlawn, with headstones for individual family members. Another family's magnificent Celtic cross rises behind.

REISINGER

The museum entrance seems guarded by an impressive bronze cast of the Lion of Brunswick (1166), but welcomes thousands of visitors each year.

HUGO (1856-1914)

German-born businessman Hugo Reisinger and his family lie within this circle of classical columns enclosing a sacred place, called a *peribolus*. Reisinger dedicated his life and fortune to promoting German-American understanding, setting himself up as a virtual one-man cultural exchange foundation. He subsidized the translation of German literary classics into English, and he sponsored touring exhibitions of German art in America and of American art in Germany. He served as a trustee of leading museums both in the United States and in Germany.

When the Nazis declared modern art "degenerate" and ridded German collections of masterpieces by German artists Max Beckmann, E. L. Kirchner, Josef Albers, and other undoubtedly great modern artists, some of these wonderful pictures were snapped up by Harvard University's Germanic Museum. Hugo Reisinger and his father-in-law, beer baron Adolphus Busch, had endowed that museum, which had opened in 1908 with additional gifts from the Kaiser himself. Today it is known as the Busch-Reisinger Museum, and its precious collections include art objects from the late-medieval period right up to the present.

Shown here in the 1953 Broadway production of "Guys and Dolls," Jack Prince, in the role of Nicely-Nicely Johnson, stopped the show with his confession of his sins in the hit "Sit Down You're Rockin' the Boat."

DAMON (1884-1946)

Damon Runyon isn't buried here. He approved of the plot and of the stone, and he saw his wife to rest here, but, as for himself, his friend World War I ace, Eddie Rickenbacker, carried out his wishes by scattering his ashes from an airplane over Runyon's beloved Broadway. Then the plane continued up to the Bronx and banked here over the family plot.

Runyon had been born in Manhattan—Manhattan, Kansas, that is, which had been founded by his grandfather. Damon first won nationwide fame as a newspaper columnist and feature writer, covering everything from horse races in Miami to electrocutions at Sing Sing, and the wars in Mexico and France. He covered trials and sporting events, sometimes brilliantly combining them, as in his classic comparison of a murderer's grip on a sashweight with the batting stance of Paul Waner, a top baseball hitter. Runyon insisted that murder was Americans' favorite sport—"the main event" he called it.

Runyon's claim to a permanent place in American literature, however, rests on his hilarious short stories of Broadway characters; gangsters, chorus girls, gamblers, bookies and broken athletes; a world of crime and violence, and dissipation, and predatory worthlessness, but off-hand decency too. The stories are all narrated in the present tense ("So he says to me . . ."), the ungrammatical purity of which is almost religiously observed. Runyon's slang is distinctive too. The words are new, but they are so clear in context that you never need a glossary. Runyon gave our language "cheaters" for glasses, "croak" for die, "dukes" for fists, "equalizer" for gun, "knock" for criticize, and countless other fresh words. Runyon cranked out his stories mechanically—almost exactly 5,000 words each for $1 per word for the leading magazines of the day. The first collection later provided the title and story line for one of the masterpieces of the American musical theatre, "Guys and Dolls," (1950, with story by Swerling and Burrows, music and lyrics by Frank Loesser).

Runyon never touched liquor, but he was a three-pack-a-day smoker, and when he eventually succumbed to cancer his pal, Walt Winchell, made a radio appeal for funds to fight the disease. Today's Damon Runyon-Walter Winchell Fund supports 150 cancer research projects each year.

Sherry's restaurant was the site of C.K.G. Billings' 1903 horseback dinner. Against a painted backdrop of rustic scenery and potted palms, guests in white tie and starched shirts ate off trays attached to pommels of saddles, while their mounts dined from a trough. Waiters in riding boots and hunting pinks doubled as grooms, sweeping up droppings between popping champagne corks.

LOUIS (1856-1926)

Architect Stanford White designed both Louis Sherry's society restaurant on Fifth Avenue and also Sherry's mausoleum at Woodlawn, seen here as a small Doric temple.

Ambitious young Vermonter Louis Sherry had first opened a small New York City confectionary shop remembered by Clarence Day as selling "delicious ice cream and French pastries and bon bons." Later Sherry hosted Society's grand dinners and balls in his palatial restaurant. Mrs. Astor's ball for 450 on January 9, 1905, is a typical entry in Sherry's leather-bound order book. At 11:00 p.m. guests arrived from rich heavy dinners all over town and sat down to a nine course midnight supper with terrapin, fish, canvasback duck, pate de foie gras, beef and champagne. With this foundation, they went upstairs to dance a cotillion, returning later for another five course supper.

Sherry experimented, submitting native American ingredients to traditional French cooking methods, thus developing a new cuisine, and he taught Americans to eat their salad. When Prohibition came, the business was no fun anymore. Sherry closed the restaurant, but later reverted to his start in business and opened a new candy store.

Elizabeth Cady Stanton, seated, met Susan B. Anthony in 1850, and for the next half-century these two were, in Stanton's words, "two sticks of a drum keeping up a rub-a-dub of agitation." Stanton was a better writer and a more popular platform speaker, but the task of raising her seven children kept her at home writing speeches for Anthony to deliver. "She forged the thunderbolts," wrote Anthony, "and I fired them." Anthony's protegee, Carrie Catt, carried on their work.

ELIZABETH CADY (1815-1902)

When Elizabeth Cady Stanton was a child she went through her father's law books with a pencil, resolving to cut out those laws which were unfair to women and made them cry. In 1848, she organized the convention in Seneca Falls, New York, which launched America's women's rights movement. Its "Declaration of Sentiments" insisted that "All men and women are created equal." For the rest of Stanton's life she articulated the movement's ideology and set its agenda, much of which remains unachieved even today in education, job training, equal wages, labor unions, birth control, property and child custody rights, and reform of divorce laws.

Stanton was a respectable matron of distinguished background and ancestry, but her thoughts were revolutionary. Before launching the women's rights movement, she energetically championed abolition; her husband, Henry B. Stanton (1805-1887) was a leading abolitionist orator. ("Obey" was, of course, omitted from their marriage vows.) When abolition and women's suffrage were not granted together after the Civil War, as many women has assumed they would be, Elizabeth's disappointment was intense, but she only redoubled her efforts in writing and speaking out. She did not live to see women's suffrage added to the Constitution in 1920, but still today we might hear her challenge, "Until every citizen shall be cloaked with all his rights and feel a personal responsibility for the nation's welfare, our republicanism, our democracy, is a sham, and our boasted experiment of self-government remains untried."

John Barrymore wrote Blanche Thomas:

> Oh, my beloved, my dearest beloved, I have
> waited and longed and prayed and cursed
> for you all my life like a marooned soul
> on a deserted coast. . . . Please, for the love of
> heaven, believe that your future is strewn
> with little pieces of my heart for your
> feet to walk on so they need not touch the
> earth. . . . I love you, I love you, I love you.

Pretty powerful stuff from the leading matinee idol of the day to
another man's wife, but it worked. Blanche divorced her husband
and married John on August 15, 1920. Diana was born on March
3, 1921. John Barrymore adored her. "You were a child of love." he
emphasized to her later.

MICHAEL (1890-1950) and her daughter
DIANA BARRYMORE (1921-1960)

Poet-playwright-actress Michael Strange (born Blanche Oelrichs) and actress
Diana Barrymore, her daughter by actor John Barrymore, lie here among Michael's
conservative upper-crust Oelrichs relations. Diana Barrymore recalled her competi-
tive, egotistical parents' tempestuous married life as "a tennis match in Hell, with
nobody missing the ball." Diana committed suicide shortly after the filming of her own
autobiography *Too Much, Too Soon*.

This photograph of the *Titanic* sailing out from Belfast on her acceptance trials in 1911 clearly betrays that her fourth smokestack was false, added only to convey the impression of size and speed. She departed from Southampton for her maiden voyage to New York on April 10, 1912 and, despite the publicity given the opulence of the ship's first class quarters, her expected profits were to come from the immigrants in steerage. The great ship sideswiped an iceberg just before midnight on April 14, 1912, and she sank at 2:20 A.M. on the 15th, taking over 1,500 passengers and crew members with her. It was the worst sea disaster to that date.

ISADOR (1845-1912) and
IDA (1849-1912)

The funeral barge in front of the Straus family mausoleum memorializes the death of Isador and Ida Straus on the *Titanic*. He wouldn't get into a lifeboat until all the women and children had been saved, and she refused to leave without him, and so they perished together. Inscribed on the back of the stone we read: "Many waters cannot quench our love—neither can the floods drown it" (*Song of Solomon* 8:7).

Architect James Gamble Rogers designed the mausoleum for the family which built Macy's into the world's largest department store. R.H. Macy himself (1822-1877), the Nantucket whaling skipper who had founded the store in 1858, lies nearby.

A Japanese aristocrat, Takamine was born in a castle in the year that the American Commodore Perry completed the treaty "opening" Japan. He chose to live and work in the United States even though American law then prevented Japanese from ever being naturalized as American citizens. His American-born wife, a direct descendant of a *Mayflower* passenger, had to surrender her American citizenship.

Doctor Takamine was a man of immense wealth and sophistication; he was a founder of both the Nippon Club and the Japan Society in New York City. Mrs. Takamine's cousin, Agnes DeMille, remembered him impressively, "About Doctor Takamine there was only awe. He was not aloof, but he was just different and superb! He walked straight into the blaze of the new century with the concept of a single world."

Shortly before his death, Doctor Takamine converted from Buddhism to Roman Catholicism and his funeral was accorded the honor of being held at Saint Patrick's Cathedral.

JOKICHI (1854-1922)

Doctor Jokichi Takamine donated the famous cherry trees which beautify Washington, D.C., and which later supplied grafts to be replanted in Tokyo after the devastation of Japan during World War II. A weeping cherry tree and a tulip tree blossom together for just a few spring days at his Woodlawn mausoleum.

Doctor Takamine earned recognition as "the father of modern biotechnology" by developing the first commercial starch-digesting enzyme in 1886, and he was also the first scientist to isolate adrenalin, in 1901.

UNTERMYER

SAMUEL (1858-1922)

Samuel Untermyer came to New York from his native Virginia soon after his father, a planter, dropped dead of a heart attack upon hearing of Lee's surrender at Appomatox. Samuel worked his way through law school, and his brilliance soon won him recognition and wealth. He counseled great corporations and financial institutions, but he was always on the look-out for any abuse of the public trust and, if he saw any, he was quick to recommend legislative remedies. He actually designed much of modern American capitalism when he served as legal counsel to public investigations which lay the groundwork for our Federal Reserve Law, the Clayton Anti-Trust Law, the Federal Trade Commission Bill, and the later Securities and Exchange Act and Glass-Steagall Banking Act.

Samuel Untermyer's lapel always sported a fresh orchid. As his orchids wilted during days of hearings in stifling Congressional hearing rooms, Untermyer aides sat by with fresh replacements in dampened paper bags. The orchids came from hothouses on Untermyer's fabulous estate in Yonkers, "Greystone." It had once been the estate of Governor Samuel Tilden, and Untermyer bequeathed it as a public park.

Lawyer Samuel Untermyer's hobby was gardening and landscaping, and his Woodlawn plot is a full quarter-acre. A fountain dominates the crest of a hill; water falls down terraces to the left, while to the right a walk over ledgerstones leads to a bronze monument by sculptor Gertrude Vanderbilt Whitney. The figures in this monument are protected on three sides by great bronze doors left open through the summer.

MADAM C J WALKER and daughter on a sight-seeing tour

A'LELIA (1885-1931)

Madam Walker's daughter, A'Lelia, shown here in the towncar with her mother, inherited one-third of her fortune (two-thirds went to charity). She emerged as the glamorous "Mahogany Millionairess," hostess and patroness of the Harlem Renaissance of the 1920's. At one party Whites were served chitterlins and bathtub gin; Blacks, caviar and champagne. A'Lelia's parties provided many talented young black musicians and writers with opportunity to move up in the world, and her pocketbook often discreetly helped out as well.

SARA B. (1867-1919)

Born in Deep South poverty, a widowed mother at nineteen, Sara Walker parlayed a hair treatment into a cosmetics empire. Madam C.J. Walker was represented from coast to coast by over 2,000 agents, and the Walker Company factory and school in Indianapolis offered training not only in beauty culture, but also in setting up a small business and keeping financial records. A generation of black entrepreneurs first found opportunity with the Walker Company.

Madam Walker was the richest self-made woman in America, and probably our first black millionaire-entrepreneur, but her personal creed remained "Lord, help me live from day to day/ In such a self-forgetful way/ That when I ever kneel to pray/ My prayers shall be for others."

Young America was "the acme of perfection" of clippers, Webb's last, and his personal favorite. "Take good care of her, mister," he said to the mate, "because after she's gone there will be no more like her." Launched in 1853, she set a Liverpool-to-San Francisco speed record for sail that still stands. She disappeared at sea in 1886. Here famed marine painter Charles Robert Patterson has envisioned her under sail.

WILLIAM (1816-1899)

Shipbuilder William Webb's graceful clipper ships "flew" passengers to California ("Flying Craft for San Francisco, Now Up," ran an 1853 New York newspaper ad) and set speed records around the world which still stand. When a Webb ship bested a Boston clipper in one famous race, waterfront rumor had it that in paying off the wagers, Boston went broke.

Webb nevertheless saw steam and iron replacing sails and wood, and so he endowed what is still today America's premier Institute of Naval Architecture.

WHITNEY FAMILY

Ambitious young William C. Whitney (1841-1904) came to New York City from his native New England in 1864, and he lost no time in building a fortune in street railways and real estate. He married another fortune, choosing Flora Payne (1842-1893), daughter of Ohio Senator Henry Payne and sister of Standard Oil partner, Oliver Payne.

Once he was rich, Whitney turned to public service. He helped to bring down the corrupt Tweed Ring and then, serving as New York City Corporate Counsel, he wrote legislation which provided a model for governing cities across America. President Grover Cleveland appointed Whitney Secretary of the Navy, and in that office Whitney fought dishonest contractors, junked worthless ships, established the Naval War College, encouraged the development of the United States steel industry, and planned and began the construction of a wholly new navy, earning recognition as the "Father of the Modern American Navy."

When Flora Whitney died in 1893, William remarried and took up a scale of living so grand that soon, in the words of Henry Adams, "New York no longer knew what most to envy, his houses or his horses." He maintained eleven houses in America and abroad, and he took special pride in his prize-winning stables and farms.

William's son, Harry (1872-1930), inherited his father's love of horses, and he played on the polo team that won the American Challenge Cup three consecutive times.

Harry Whitney married Gertrude Vanderbilt (1875-1942), an extraordinary woman who led two very different lives. Uptown she was indisputably an aristocrat, a dignified society matron who won a highly-publicized court battle for custody of her niece, Gloria Vanderbilt. Downtown in Bohemian Greenwich Village, however, Gertrude Vanderbilt Whitney was recognized as an artist, an important American sculptor. Her colossal statue of Buffalo Bill stands in Cody, Wyoming, at the approach to Yellowstone Park, and in Washington, D.C. we can see her Titanic Memorial in Potomac Park and her Aztec Fountain in the Pan-American Building. She sculpted a memorial to commemorate the first landing of American troops in Europe during World War I; this perched high on a cliff over the beach at Saint Nazaire, France, until the Nazis deliberately destroyed it during World War II. Gertrude's work graces the Untermyer plot here at Woodlawn.

Gertrude created art and collected it too and, in 1929, she offered a collection of over 600 modern American paintings plus other works to New York's Metropolitan Museum of Art, complete with a generous endowment to build and maintain a wing to display American art. The art wasn't then appreciated, however, and so the Museum turned down the gift. Gertrude went ahead and built a museum on her own, The Whitney Museum of American Art. Today that Museum not only displays a rich selection of American art at its Madison Avenue home, but has established branch museums throughout New York City and suburbs, and has a generous reputation of nationwide lending.

The Whitney family monument of highly polished black granite with decorative bronze swags and lettering was designed by society architect Stanford White in the form of an ancient Greek crowned stele. The planting of shrubs over the individual gravesites echoes an ancient Levantine custom which may be seen in cemeteries in Greece, Turkey and throughout the Near East.

William C. Whitney earned his epithet "Father of the Modern American Navy" by ending graft and mismanagement and by launching a rebuilding program during his tenure as Navy Secretary from 1885 to 1889. Cartoonist Thomas Nast popularized Whitney's reforms. (*Harper's Weekly*, December 19, 1885)

THE REMEDY FOUND.
COMMANDER WHITNEY. "Substantially thrown away!"

Gertrude Vanderbilt Whitney patronized all aspects of modern art, and here she models one of Leon Bakst's stage costumes. The only time that Gertrude's "Uptown Society life" and "Downtown Bohemian life" came together was the 1913 Armory Modern Art Show, of which she was a principal sponsor. She designed and paid for the decorations, and she chose the show's symbol, the pine tree flag of the American Revolution.

Masonic symbols ornament Bert Williams' tombstone. Following a funeral service at Saint Philip's Protestant Episcopal Church, the Saint Cecilia Masonic Lodge 568 held the first Masonic services in New York State for a black man, as Williams had wished. In his coffin were placed the traditional lambskin and the sprig of acacia, symbolizing the Masons' faith in the immortality of the soul.

BERT (1873-1922)

Bert Williams made American stage history as the first major black performer on Broadway. "He was the funniest man I ever saw," said W. C. Fields, "and the saddest man I ever knew." Williams' sorrow was rooted in "my listening to the applause of the audience every night, but then having to take the freight elevator home."

Williams was born on the Caribbean Island of Antigua, but he moved to California as a child, and, there in 1895, teamed up with George Walker, a Kansas-born seasoned minstrel performer. The two created a comedy song and dance act in which Walker, as a prancing dandy, played against Williams as a slow-witted, shuffling, traditional "darkie." They brought this act to New York in 1896 and billed themselves as "Two Real Coons," because white entertainers were winning audiences with minstrel-type shows in blackface. Williams himself had to wear blackface, because he was naturally quite light-skinned. Williams and Walker introduced and popularized the cake-walk, and in 1902, they opened the first major Broadway musical written and performed by blacks, "In Dahomey." This ragtime musical was a smash hit in New York and later in London, where they performed at the ninth birthday party for the Prince of Wales (later Duke of Windsor). Other joint successes followed until Walker's retirement in 1907.

By then Williams was already receiving a generous income as one of the first and most popular singing voices recorded, but from 1910 to 1919 he won even greater fame in the Ziegfield Follies. The first black entertainer to headline an integrated show, he performed solo skits and songs, and he appeared on stage with white actors, but he was never allowed to be onstage with a white actress.

Williams collapsed from overwork and died at the age of 46 in 1922. By that time Charles Gilpin had won recognition as the first black serious actor on Broadway, appearing as the Emperor Jones, but Williams had opened the door for Gilpin, and for all of the other great black actors and entertainers who have moved us and amused us right up to Bill Cosby today.

"Battle Cry" might well have been the title of a biography of Barbara Hutton herself. Her beauty and riches won her insistent media attention first as a "poor little rich girl" in the Depression years and then through a series of notably unhappy marriages.

F. W. (1852-1919)

F. W. Woolworth discovered that by displaying merchandise attractively, and by keeping prices low, fixed, and in convenient coins, customers could be induced to buy on impulse. His successful formula built up a chain of over 1,000 stores by the time of his death, caused by septic poisoning when he refused to pay to see a dentist.

Woolworth's granddaughter, Barbara Hutton (1912-1979) derisively dubbed her grandfather's mausoleum "the pyramid," but she joined him there in death. The Egyptian-revival style tomb compares with that of Jules Bache, which it faces across Woodlawn's Central Avenue. Both were designed by architect John Russell Pope, who later designed the Jefferson Memorial in Washington, D.C.

Other Notables in Brief

Only a multivolume encyclopedia could profile all of the interesting or famous people interred at Woodlawn. I have not yet mentioned a number of families who are virtual household names in America such as the Harpers and the Scribners (publishing), Hertzes (car rental), Berkeys (with a camera-and-film decorative motif on their mausoleum), Lorillards ("Newport" cigarettes and other tobacco products; the New York Botanical Garden was once their estate and snuff mill), Wittnauers (watches), and DuPont's (chemicals). Here is a brief sampling of still a few more notables:

ALLAIRE, ANTHONY 1829-1903

Scion of a famous New York family of marine engine builders, young Anthony rose to the rank of Brigadier General in the Civil War. The family's iron mines and charcoal works gave birth to today's Allaire, New Jersey.

ALLEN, VIVIAN BEAUMONT 1885-1962

This patroness of theatre in New York City unfortunately did not live to see her last public gift completed; the theatre at Lincoln Center which bears her name opened just after her death. Mrs. Allen's father, J. E. Beaumont, had founded the May Company department stores.

ARBUCKLE, ROSCOE "FATTY" 1887-1933

Arbuckle was the grownup fat-boy of hilarious silent screen slapstick comedies, a popular favorite until involved in a 1921 scandal in which a girl died. He later directed a few pictures under the name of William Goodrich.

BERGH, HENRY 1811-1888

Bergh was the founder of the American Society for the Prevention of Cruelty to Animals (1866) and, later, among the founders of the Society for the Prevention of Cruelty to Children (1875).

CORNELIUS BLISS and FAMILY

Industrialist Cornelius Bliss (1833-1911) was Secretary of the Interior in President McKinley's first administration, and, had he not declined the vice-presidential nomination in 1900, he instead of Teddy Roosevelt would have become president when McKinley was assassinated in 1901. Cornelius Bliss, Jr. (1874-1949) followed his father's lead in industry (textiles), and politics, serving as treasurer of the National Republican Party. Daughter Lizzie (1864-1931) became an art patroness; her collection formed the nucleus of the Museum of Modern Art, of which she was a founder in 1929.

BOLDT, GEORGE C. 1851-1916

As President of the Waldorf-Astoria Hotel Company, Boldt was more responsible than any other man for the modern American luxury hotel. He made the name of his hotel synonymous with elegance by insisting that there would always be people willing to pay "high prices for good things."

BORDEN, MATTHEW C.D. 1842-1912

Borden's cotton mills and cotton printing plants, the world's largest, in Fall River, Massachusetts, earned him the title "The King of Calico."

BOSTWICK, JABEZ 1831-1892

Bostwick was a founder and original partner in Standard Oil Company. He died in the collapse of a burning stable at his Long Island estate when he was trying to rescue the horses.

BRICKTOP 1895-1984

Who would recognize the name Ada Beatrice Queen Victoria Louise Virginia Smith Duconge for this fabled jazz club hostess and singer?

BRISTOW, BENJAMIN HELM 1832-1896

Bristow fought bravely alongside U.S. Grant at several major Civil War battles, and he was later appointed by Grant to be the United States' first Solicitor General (1870-1872). Bristow subsequently served as Grant's Secretary of the Treasury (1874-76), cleaning up several scandals in that department, and in 1879 he was elected the second president of the American Bar Association.

BULOVA, ARDE 1889-1958

Everybody knows of Bulova's watches, but Arde Bulova was also a leader in scientific and technical research and instrumentation, and in the development of training and employment programs for the handicapped.

BURRELL, DR. DAVID J. 1844-1926

As the minister at New York's famous Marble Collegiate Church from 1891 until his death, and as Director of the Anti-Saloon League of America, Doctor Burrell was one of the principals behind the shortlived "achievement" of Prohibition in the United States.

BUSTEED, RICHARD 1822-1898

When President Lincoln appointed Busteed U.S. District Judge for recently-conquered Alabama in 1863, Busteed preserved the principle of independent counsel in the United States by daring to overturn as unconstitutional a federal law requiring lawyers practicing before federal courts to take loyalty oaths. The Supreme Court upheld his ruling in the spring of 1867, infuriating a Congress determined to punish the South. Busteed had earlier served as Corporate Council for the City of New York (1856-1859) and, during his military service during the Civil War, he had risen to the rank of General.

BUTLER, CHARLES 1802-1897

At the time of prominent attorney Charles Butler's death, he was president of both the University of the City of New York (later to be New York University) and of Union Theological Seminary. Benjamin Franklin Butler was his brother, and his wife was the sister of William Ogden.

CHAPIN, ALFRED CLARK 1848-1936

This prominent member of an old-line Puritan family (Augustus Saint Gaudens' famous statue "The Puritan" was based on an ancestor) served as mayor of the independent city of Brooklyn (1888-1891) and member of Congress (1891-92).

CLARK, HORACE F. 1815-1873

Horace Clark served two terms in the United States Congress (1854-1858), but, as the son-in-law of Commodore Vanderbilt, he withdrew from politics to concentrate on the family's many railroad interests. He was a founding trustee of Woodlawn Cemetery.

CLEWS, HENRY 1834-1923

During the Civil War, Clews' bank was second only to that of Cooke and Company as agents of the public business of the United States Treasury and financiers of the Union. Later Henry was a financial advisor to Japan, and decorated by that government.

CORBIN, AUSTIN 1827-1896

Corbin financed both the development of Coney Island and the construction of the Long Island Railroad, but he had gotten his start in business out in Iowa. His First National Bank of Davenport was the first to open its doors under the 1863 legislation which created the national bank system.

CROMWELL, WILLIAM NELSON 1854-1948

William Cromwell played an important, but shadowy role in the financing of the American-sponsored 1903 civil war in Colombia. During that war, the Panama area of Colombia seceded from Colombia, and the United States immediately recognized it as independent so that we could build a canal across the isthmus. Later Cromwell, trained as both a lawyer and an accountant, would earn the title "the physician of Wall Street" for his shrewdness in devising legal reorganizations to save financially ailing corporations. Manhattan's prestigious law firm Sullivan and Cromwell survives today.

CULLEN, COUNTEE 1903-1946

Cullen was a major American poet whose lyrics often echo his idol, John Keats. Helen Keller wrote him, "Your poetry has magic to turn my prison-house into a Garden of Delight." Senegalese poet-president, Leopold Senghor, specified Cullen among black Americans whose works inspired racial pride throughout colonial Africa.

DAMROSCH, DR. LEOPOLD 1832-1885

Founder of the New York Oratorio Society (1873), the New York Symphony (1878; today the Philharmonic), and of a virtual dynasty of musicians and music teachers, Damrosch earned his title "Doctor" in the study of medicine in his native Germany; only much later did Columbia University give him an honorary doctorate in music. Lincoln Center's Damrosch Park is today the site of free outdoor concerts.

DEAS, ZACHARIAH 1819-1882

Deas was born into a leading South Carolina family, but he lost his fortune during the Civil War while he won distinction as a general and one of the great heroes of the Confederacy. He fought at the battles of Murfreesboro, Chickamauga, and Missionary Ridge. After the War he came to New York and quietly rebuilt his fortune trading cotton.

DeKOVEN, REGINALD 1859-1920 and
ANNA FARWELL 1869-1953

DeKoven composed many of America's most popular turn-of-the-century operettas and set us on the path toward independent development of the American stage musical. His one supremely beautiful score, *Robin Hood*, included the song "Oh Promise Me," which has so long been a standard at weddings that Julie Andrews surprised movie audiences when she sang it at a funeral in the 1980 film *S.O.B.*

Anna Farwell DeKoven wrote successful novels, historical studies, and biographies, and her translations of French novels remain definitive.

DELAFIELD FAMILY

John Delafield, of Fieldston Manor, England, was the head of one of England's oldest families. He came to New York in 1783, married an American lady, and stayed to go into business as a merchant and private underwriter. The Delafields were among the richest people in the city, with a great mansion on Manhattan's southern tip, the Battery, and a great country estate, Sunswick, along the East River in today's borough of Queens. The Delafields had nine sons, one of whom, Major Joseph Delafield (1790-1875) fought bravely in the War of 1812, and then served on the post-war commission which finally settled the Minnesota-Canadian border, an issue which had rankled British-American relations since the Revolution. Major Joseph owned substantial tracts in the Bronx, where he built himself an American "Fieldston Manor," today's elegant Fieldston residential district. Major Joseph's son Lewis (1834-1883) was a founder of the Society for the Prevention of Cruelty to Children. Delafield descendants continued to distinguish themselves through the generations.

DODGE, WILLIAM 1805-1883

Dry goods merchant, William Dodge, married Melissa Phelps in 1828 and went into business with his wealthy father-in-law to build the enormous metals conglomerate, Phelps-Dodge Corporation. William was a founder of the Young Men's Christian Association (1851) and a member of Congress (1866-1868).

DREICER FAMILY

Where did Diamond Jim Brady get his diamonds? At Dreicer's, of course! Jacob Dreicer (1840-1921) founded the family jewelry store on Fifth Avenue and opened a branch at Saratoga during the summer season of horse racing, gambling and taking the waters there. Jacob's son, Michael (1868-1921), made pearls fashionable in High Society; they had previously been thought unlucky. The Metropolitan Museum's precious Dreicer Collection of Gothic and early Renaissance artworks was Michael's bequest.

EHRET, GEORGE 1835-1927

German immigrant George Ehret founded his Hell Gate Brewery in 1867 and quickly built it into one of the world's largest. He lost it as Alien Property during World War I, recovered it when he became an American citizen, but soon had to convert it to the production of near beer during prohibition. Ehret's French-style mausoleum is one of the most impressive at Woodlawn.

FAHNESTOCK, HARRIS C. 1835-1914

As a young man, Fahnestock ran Jay Cooke's Washington, D.C. office during the Civil War, when Cooke's was the number one financial agent of the federal government. Later Fahnestock moved to New York and took up a position among leading bankers here.

FLAGLER, JOHN HALDANE 1836-1922 and
ALICE MANDELICK 1842-1918

John Flagler invented and supplied many of the pumps and pipes to America's young oil industry. His National Tube Company eventually became a part of United States Steel. His wife, a famed contralto, won his heart (and his $20 million) with her rendition of the "Flower Song" from the opera *Faust*.

FOSTER, WILLIAM F. 1841-1895

Foster built up a fortune in Chicago real estate, only to lose that in the great fire of 1871. He came to New York and established a second fortune with Foster's Glove Fasteners Company.

FOX, RICHARD K. 1846-1922

Fox's *National Police Gazette*, "the Bible of the barbershop," featured lurid crimes, sports, and theatrical gossip, with plenty of illustrations of decolleté actresses and women acrobats in tights. "Be interesting!" Fox exhorted his writers, "and be quick about it!" Fox was a dandy who never played any games or sports, or even learned the rules to any, but his paper virtually created America's distinctive sports culture.

FRISCH, FRANK 1898-1973

Playing with the New York Giants and the Saint Louis Cardinals, "the Fordham Flash" hit over .300 in 13 of his 19 seasons. Casey Stengel said, "Then there was Mr. Frisch, who went to a university and could run fast besides."

GARRISON, LINDLEY MILLER 1864-1932

Garrison was a prominent New Jersey attorney and a friend of Woodrow Wilson when Wilson appointed him Secretary of War in 1913. He resigned in 1916 over Wilson's refusal to support a strong national defense establishment, but his legacy was our preparedness for war when we did join World War I, the next year.

GIGLIO, CLEMENTE 1886-1943

Naples-born Giglio was the leader of the Italian-American theatre, writing and acting in over 100 plays, including an Italian version of *Uncle Tom's Cabin*.

GREGOR, ELMER T. 1880-1954

Gregor wrote 28 children's books about American Indians, the most popular of which were *The Red Arrow* and the "Jim Mason" series, based on authentic incidents from the French and Indian War. He founded the Buckskin Men of America, a forerunner of the Boy Scouts.

HAMMERSTEIN, OSCAR 1847-1919 and son,
ARTHUR 1872-1955

With the profits from the cigar-making machinery he invented at age 18, Oscar Hammerstein opened vaudeville and variety theatres, earning his tag, "The Father of Times Square." His real love however, was opera. Jokers said that every Saturday night a wagon took the profits from his vaudeville house to make up the deficit at his opera house, and they weren't far from the truth. Hammerstein's Opera Company gave the Metropolitan its only serious competition until the Met, drawing on the limitless resources of New York Society, bought him out. Arthur followed his father into the business, and Oscar's love of music was also inherited by his grandson, Oscar Hammerstein II (buried in California).

HARRIS, CHARLES KASSELL 1865-1930

Harris was a songwriter whose most popular tune, "After the Ball is Over" (1892), reputedly sold over 5 million copies in the 1890's.

HAVEMEYER, WILLIAM F. 1804-1874

William retired from the family's sugar refining business at age 38 and entered politics, serving as mayor of New York in 1845-46, 1848-49 and again in 1873-74.

HECKSCHER, AUGUST 1848-1941

This German immigrant acquired great wealth developing coal, zinc and other mines. Many will remember that his grandson and namesake became the New York City Commissioner of Parks in the administration of Mayor John Lindsay.

HELD, JOHN 1889-1958

Held was the pre-eminent illustrator of "The Jazz Age," illustrating F. Scott Fitzgerald's book which gave the age its name. His figures are recognizable at once: girls with a boyish bob, a turned up nose, a winsome expression, thin long legs, and stylish clothes; his men: a spherical head, brilliantined hair, dots for eyes, stick necks, huge feet and hands and, of course, equally stylish threads.

HERTER, CHRISTIAN 1840-1883 and his son,
CHRISTIAN A. 1865-1910

Christian Herter was the decorator and designer to Gilded Age High Society. Articles of furniture which he designed and made are treasured museum pieces today.

His son built one of the first biochemical laboratories in the United States and counted among those who developed medical education and research in America from relative obscurity to world leadership. Herter was appointed to the first Food and Drug Administration Board, and he founded, edited and even subsidized the important *Journal of Biological Chemistry.*

HOLLS, FREDERICK 1857-1903 and father,
GEORGE 1824-1886

Frederick Holls convinced President McKinley that the United States ought to be represented at the International Peace Conference at the Hague, Holland, in 1899 and, once there, Holls lobbied so effectively for an international arbitration tribunal that the nations agreed to set one up. Holls won recognition as the "father" of the

148

Permanent Court of Arbitration, predecessor to all twentieth century international institutions.

Frederick's father, George, also buried here, was a German immigrant Lutheran pastor who founded some of the first orphanages across the United States.

HUDNUT, RICHARD ALEXANDER 1855-1928

This perfume manufacturer's famous line of cosmetics long survived his death, and eventually merged with today's Warner-Lambert Corporation.

HYDE, HENRY B. 1834-1898 and son,
JAMES H. 1876-1959

Henry Hyde founded the Equitable in 1859 and soon built it into the country's largest life insurance company by assiduously training his sales force, transforming salesmanship into a profession. Henry's son, James, inherited control of the Equitable, but his flamboyant lifestyle, tagged "High Life Insurance" by the press, touched off investigations of possible financial improprieties, and these investigations inspired new regulations of the industry.

KNAPP, HERMAN 1832-1911

Doctor Herman Knapp was already famous in Europe as a physician and eye surgeon when he came to New York and opened an Eye and Ear Institute here. The care he provided (often free), plus his teaching, writing and inventing new surgical instruments and techniques extended his influence. *The Journal of Ophthalmology*, which he founded in 1869, continues today under the auspices of the American Medical Association.

LAMONT, DANIEL S. 1851-1905

After serving as private secretary to President Cleveland in Cleveland's first term (1885-1889), Lamont was recalled as Secretary of War in the second Cleveland administration (1893-1897). His business partnerships with William C. Whitney between and after his periods of government service made him a wealthy man.

LAUNITZ, BARON ROBERT 1808-1870

While one of Baron Launitz's brothers became a bishop, and all four others became generals in the Imperial Russian Army, Baron Robert went to Rome to study sculpture under the great Thorvaldsen, and then migrated to America to practice his art. His most famous works are the Civil War monument in Frankfort, Kentucky, and the Pulaski Monument in Savannah, Georgia.

LECOMTE DeNOUY, PIERRE 1883-1947

This biophisicist, inventor, and scientist authored popular books (notably *Human Destiny*, 1947) which tried to reconcile science with religious belief.

LEHMAN FAMILY

Bavarian immigrant Henry Lehman opened a crockery shop in Montgomery, Alabama in 1845, thus founding an American business dynasty still familiar in the name of giant Shearson-Lehman-American Express Company. When Henry's brothers arrived, they expanded into cotton trading and then banking in New Orleans and New York City. Family leadership eventually passed on to Henry's nephew, Philip (1861-1947) who helped launch Sears, Roebuck Company, F.W. Woolworth, and other major corporations. Philip's son, Robert (1891-1969) later backed the airline, electronics, and motion picture industries. Father and son assembled a fabulous art collection which is today housed in the special Lehman Pavilion of the Metropolitan Museum of Art.

McADOO, WILLIAM 1853-1930

McAdoo led a varied career of service as Congressman, Assistant Secretary of the Navy for Grover Cleveland, Police Commissioner of New York City, and eventually Chief New York City magistrate until his death.

McMANUS, GEORGE 1884-1954

McManus introduced his comic characters, Maggie and Jiggs, in the strip "Bringing Up Father" in 1913. At its peak, the strip was enjoyed by 80 million readers in 46 countries, in 16 languages.

MARCANTONIO, VITO ANTHONY 1902-1954

Vito Marcantonio represented East Harlem in Congress from 1934-1936 and 1938-1951. His campaigns for civil rights, for public ownership of utilities, and for increasing taxes on the rich were considered too radical by many. His acting as attorney for the American Communist Party in 1951 was for many the last straw. He lies at Woodlawn just a few yards from his mentor, Fiorello LaGuardia.

MOORE, JOHN BASSETT 1860-1947

In 1903 President Roosevelt was scrounging for any legal excuse to seize the isthmus of Panama in order to build a canal. Moore gave him one based in an 1846 treaty with Colombia, and Roosevelt's subsequent message to Congress was, wrote Roosevelt to Moore, "as much yours as mine." Moore later served as the first American judge on the World Court.

MORTON, PAUL 1857-1911

Morton served as Secretary of the Navy for just one year (1904), but stepped down to accept the position of Chairman of the Board of the Equitable Life Assurance Company and rehabilitate that corporation after the James Hyde years.

NAGLE, DR. JOHN T. 1854-1919

Dr. Nagle was a close friend and associate of Jacob Riis, the author of *How the*

Other Half Lives, and together they fought for city parks in poor districts, for a ban on the renting of rear tenements without windows or air, and for other important health and housing legislation.

NAUMBURG, WALTER 1867-1959

This eminent banker paid for the Naumburg Band Shell in Central Park and for a regular series of free public concerts.

NEWMAN, WILLIAM H. 1847-1918

Newman planned and oversaw the construction of Grand Central Station as President of the New York Central Railroad from 1901-1909.

NYE, JAMES W. 1814-1876

President Lincoln appointed this prominent New York Republican supporter Governor of the newly created Nevada Territory (1861-1864); Nye later served as Senator when Nevada became a state (1864-1873). Nye County is just outside Las Vegas.

OLCOTT, CHAUNCEY 1860-1932

Olcott, an Irish actor and singer in sentimental and romantic comedies, won immortality by writing "My Wild Irish Rose."

OLIVER, JOSEPH "KING" 1885-1938

This brilliant cornetist and bandleader developed New Orleans jazz and brought it north to Chicago. Long after his death his protege Louis Armstrong would still insist, "No one in jazz has created as much music as he has."

PENDELTON, ALICE KEY (1824-1886)

Francis Scott Key's daughter rests under a simple ledger stone.

PERRY FRUEAUFF, ANTOINETTE "TONY" 1888-1946

Tony Perry first won fame as an actress in her native Denver, but retired from the stage during the years of a happy marriage. She returned to the stage upon the death of her husband in 1922, and later enjoyed success as a Broadway producer and director. In 1947, in commemoration of her service, the American Theatre Wing inaugurated its annual presentation of "Tonys" for Broadway performances, staging, directing and other achievement. "Tonys" are Broadway's equivalent of Hollywood's "Oscars."

POLK, DR. WILLIAM M. 1844-1918

Polk served as a prominent military officer in the Confederate Army (his father was a Confederate general *and* the Episcopal Bishop of Louisiana!). Later, as Doctor of Obstetrics and Gynecology at the University of the City of New York and as Dean of the Cornell Medical School, Doctor Polk reorganized medical education in the United States and brought new concern and focus on women's diseases.

POPE, GENEROSO 1891-1950

Generoso Pope arrived in America at age 13 and got his first job carrying drinking water to construction workers for $3 per week. He rose to construction supervisor and, eventually, owner of the largest sand and gravel company in the New York region. His 1928 purchase of the newspaper *Il Progresso* made him a leading spokesman on national and international issues for the Italian-American community, and he became a friend and confidant of politicians right up to the White House. The Pope publishing empire is today carried on by his son, Generoso, Jr., who also owns *The Enquirer*.

POST, GEORGE B. 1837-1913

Post was a protege of architect Richard M. Hunt. Post's own works include the New York Stock Exchange, the Wisconsin State Capitol building and the buildings of the City College Campus in New York City.

PRIME, REVEREND SAMUEL I. 1812-1885

Prime's columns in the *New York Observer* and *Harper's* magazine regularly reached an estimated 100,000 readers for almost 40 years, featuring homilies, humorous anecdotes with moral lessons and thoughts on child rearing. He also campaigned for prison reform, promoting the separation of the hardened criminals from the more probably reformable, and his introduction of reading lessons for the illiterate at Sing Sing so impressed Alexis De Tocqueville that De Tocqueville introduced a similar program back in France.

RAND, JOHN GOFFE 1801-1873

Rand invented the screw-top compressible paint tube for artists, and it eventually gave us the toothpaste tube as well. He was a noted portrait painter who studied under Samuel Morse and later worked in Boston, Charleston, New York and London. William Cullen Bryant was a pallbearer at Rand's funeral.

REIK, THEODORE 1888-1969

In 1948, this Freudian psychologist founded the National Psychological Association for psychoanalysis. His many popular books include *The Secret Self* (1952) and *Of Love and Lust* (1957).

RICE, HENRY GRANTLAND 1880-1954

Rice was one of America's most popular sports journalists, successfully conveying the thrill of the contests through his distinctive "gee whiz" style of writing. His enthusiasm for sports carried him to poetic heights:
> "When the One Great Scorer comes
> To mark against your name,
> He writes - not that you won or lost -
> But how you played the game."

RICHARDS, VINCENT 1903-1959

Richards won the gold medal in the 1924 Olympic tennis singles competition, the only time the sport was ever included in the Olympics. Through his career Richards won altogether 27 national tennis titles in singles, and, often together with "Big Bill" Tilden, doubles and mixed doubles competition from the early 1920's through the late 1940's.

ROBERTS, MARSHALL O. 1814-1880

Roberts was a leading capitalist of his day, and one of the least savory. Historian Gustavus Myers writes that a Congressional investigation of his Civil War profiteering brought forth "facts that amazed and sickened a committee accustomed to ordinary political corruption." Politicians of both parties, nevertheless, always knew him as a generous contributor.

ROOS, DELMAR G. 1889-1960

The Willys Jeep, designed by Delmar Roos in 1938, proved to be the most important tactical vehicle of World War II. Millions of GI's wanted one when they got home, starting Americans' on-going love affair with "recreational vehicles."

RUBINSTEIN, SERGE 1908-1955

The murder of this shadowy Russian-born financier in his Fifth Avenue mansion made front-page news, and it remains one of New York City's most mysterious unsolved crimes.

SCHAEFER, RUDOLPH J. 1863-1923

New York's Schaefer Brewing Company was long one of America's largest, and Rudolph, the second generation in the business, won the epithet, "The father of bottled beer."

SMITH, FRANCIS HOPKINSON 1838-1915

This fine artist, whose watercolors are still held in high regard today, was also one of the leading novelists of his day. Additionally, working at his trade as a civil engineer, he designed and built the base of the Statue of Liberty.

SQUIER, EPHRAIM G. 1821-1888

The Smithsonian Institution's first publications were E. G. Squier's important studies of archaeological remains of American Indian civilizations, both in North America and in Central and South America, where Squier held several diplomatic posts. He later went to work for Frank Leslie, but he literally lost his mind when his wife, Miriam, divorced him in order to marry the boss, and died in a mental hospital.

STEDMAN, EDMUND CLARENCE 1833-1908

Stedman wrote Abraham Lincoln's first campaign song ("Honest Abe of the

West") and went on to earn distinction not only as a poet, but also as an editor, anthologizer and professor of poetry. He encouraged and even subsidized writers as diverse as Herman Melville, Emma Lazarus, and Theodore Dreiser. When he died he was the "grand old man of American letters," and newspapers quoted Samuel Clemens (Mark Twain), "His loss stuns me and unfits me to speak." Stedman's tombstone quotes poet John Greenleaf Whittier's dedication of a book to him; "Poet and Friend of Poets."

STELLA, JOSEPH 1877-1946

Italian-born Joseph Stella became America's most important futurist painter. He captured the romance of engineering: skyscrapers, subways, bridges and other visual archetypes of the New World.

STILLMAN, JAMES 1850-1918

Stillman, a native of Texas, followed his father onto the New York Cotton Exchange and eventually, through a variety of business partnerships with Rockefellers and Harrimans, rose to the presidency of the National City Bank and recognition as one of the dozen richest men in the country. His surprisingly modest Woodlawn plot reflects his secretive personality.

STRANSKY, JOSEF 1879-1936

This Prague-born musician and composer conducted the New York Philharmonic from 1911 to 1923.

TAYLOR, LAURETTE 1884-1946 and her husband
MANNERS, J. HARTLEY 1870-1928

Laurette Taylor captured American and English hearts at the beginning of her career in "Peg O' My Heart" (1912) and enjoyed equal success at the end in "The Glass Menagerie" (1945). J. Hartley Manners was the playwright who created Peg for her. Manners, an Englishman, had originally come to America as a member of Lillie Langtry's theatre company.

TILGHMAN, LLOYD 1816-1863

As a scion of Maryland's aristocratic Tilghman family, Lloyd quickly rose to the rank of General in the Confederate Armies. He fought heroically at the Battle of Vicksburg, but he was killed in action at the battle of Champion's Hill, Mississippi, on May 16, 1863. He is remembered in Paducah, Kentucky, with an impressive public monument.

VAN CORTLANDT FAMILY

Dutch soldier Oloff van Cortlandt arrived in New Amsterdam in 1638, and he amassed widespread landholdings which his descendants held for generations. Today's 1,100 acre Van Cortlandt Park in the Bronx was once part of the family's estates, and it was in the family's old burial vault there that Augustus Van Cortlandt hid New York City's municipal records during the Revolutionary War. In 1889, however, the Van Cortlandt family donated these properties for a public park, and the Van Cortlandts bought space and moved over to nearby Woodlawn.

VANDERBILT, VIRGINIA FAIR 1877-1935

Born "the princess of San Francisco," daughter of James Fair, who had won immense wealth as a partner in Virginia City's silver Comstock Lode, Virginia married William K. Vanderbilt, and together they won fame sponsoring America's first automobile races. The Vanderbilt's divorced in 1927, and when their son died in a racing accident in 1933, Virginia retired into almost complete seclusion. She lies at Woodlawn just a few yards from her sister, Theresa, who had married into the prominent Oelrichs family. (William Vanderbilt was Alva Smith Vanderbilt Belmont's son; see also the notes on Michael Strange, born Blanche Oelrichs)

VERMILYE FAMILY

Isaac Vermilye, a Walloon, settled in Upper Manhattan in 1663, and the family has played a prominent role in New York City since. Manhattan's Vermilyea Avenue records a variant spelling.

WEBB, JAMES WATSON 1802-1884

Webb's *New York Courier and Enquirer* was once America's largest newspaper, and Webb was a major figure on the stage of American political life from the age of President Jackson to that of President Hayes. Eventually his two assistants, James Bennett and Henry Raymond, founded their own papers which overshadowed his: *The Herald* and *The Times*.

WEBER, JAKE 1875-1950

Weber was the almost legendary trainer of the American Olympic Track and Field Teams for 1920, 1924, 1928, 1932, 1936 and 1948. Obituaries noted that his mausoleum was his great pride; he had it built well before he died and had it inscribed "In Memory of Jake Weber," just to be certain that he would not be forgotten. He hasn't been.

WESTINGHOUSE, HENRY H. 1853-1933

Henry was a younger brother of George, who ran the family electric company, but Henry himself was a successful inventor, notably of the single action steam engine.

WILLS, HARRY 1889-1958

The Harry Wills-Jack Dempsey fight for the heavyweight boxing championship of the world is the most famous sporting event in American history that never happened. Wills was the leading contender for Dempsey's crown, but promoters feared the racial implications of a possible Wills victory. "I was convinced," wrote Dempsey in his memoirs, "that not one of us had any integrity left." Wills won wide recognition, nevertheless, as the unofficial black heavyweight champion, "the brown panther," with an official lifetime record of 62 wins (42 by knockout) and 8 losses in 102 fights. He was elected to boxing's Hall of Fame in 1970.

WOODWARD FAMILY

The Woodward family was just another rich old New York clan (Hanover National Bank) known mostly for its polo and racehorses (Nashua) until William, Jr. (1920-1955), was shot to death by his wife, providing a plot both for Truman Capote's short story "La Cote Basque" and for Domenick Dunne's novel, later filmed, *The Two Mrs. Grenvilles*. Was the shooting an accident?

YOUMANS, EDWARD 1821-1887 and his brother,
WILLIAM 1838-1901

The Youman brothers devoted their lives to the diffusion of scientific knowledge in the United States. Each wrote several popular books and textbooks, and together they founded and edited *Popular Science Monthly* magazine, later *Scientific Monthly*.

ZIEGLER, WILLIAM 1843-1905

Ziegler's Royal Baking Powder Company was the basis of a generous fortune, much of which he spent sponsoring polar expeditions.

Some Major American Architects and A Few of Their Designs at Woodlawn

CHARLES I. BERG
Coster Mausoleum
Berg designed the 77th Street facade of the American Museum of Natural History.

THEODORE E. BLAKE
Harbeck Mausoleum (page 18)
S.H. and R.H. Kress Mausoleum
Blake worked with Carrere and Hastings on the Church of Saint Mary, Manhattanville and on the New York Public Libary.

ROBERT CATERSON
C.P. Huntington Mausoleum (page 83)
Caterson designed and built literally thousands of mausoleums around the country, including that of Huntington's partner, Leland Stanford, in Palo Alto, California. The bronze door was designed by Herbert Adams.

DUNCAN CHANDLER
Joseph Pulitzer Monument, with a bronze figure by William O. Partridge. (page 113)

H.Q. FRENCH
Jay Gould Mausoleum (page 69)
This firm originated today's Fred French Design/Realty Company.

RICHARD MORRIS HUNT or his sons, the firm of **HUNT AND HUNT**
O.H.P. and Alva Belmont Mausoleum (page 29)
Clyde Fitch Monument (page 63)
Other famous works by Hunt include several of the Newport "cottages" and the base of the Statue of Liberty. There is a memorial to R.M. Hunt himself on Fifth Avenue at 70th Street.

JARDINE, KENT AND JARDINE
G.P. Morosini Mausoleum
Their Church of the Incarnation still stands on Madison Avenue at 35th Street.

McKIM, MEAD AND WHITE

Charles J. Osborn Mausoleum
H. A. C. Taylor Mausoleum
Twombly Monument (in collaboration with L. C. Tiffany)
Goelet Mausoleum
Henry Russell Mausoleum
Louis Sherry Mausoleum (page 121)
John Sterling Mausoleum (page 17)
William C. Whitney Monument (page 137)

JOHN RUSSELL POPE

William B. Leeds Mausoleum
Garvan Mausoleum (page 65)
Woolworth Mausoleum (page 141)
Bache Mausoleum (page 27)
William C. Stewart Mausoleum

Pope's other works include the Central Park facade of the American Museum of Natural History in New York and, in Washington, the Jefferson Memorial and the National Gallery of Art.

JAMES RENWICK

Armour Mausoleum (page 25)

Renwick's other works include, in New York, Saint Patrick's Cathedral and Grace Church and, in Washington, the Smithsonian Institution.

JAMES GAMBLE ROGERS

Harkness Mausoleum (page 77)
Straus Mausoleum (page 127)

Rogers' other works include the Butler Library at Columbia University, the Columbia-Presbyterian medical Center, the Yale Club in New York and the Harkness Buildings at Yale in New Haven.

LOUIS COMFORT TIFFANY

Cohan Mausoleum (page 43)
Webb Mausoleum (page 135)
Twombly Monument (in collaboration with McKim, Mead and White)

YORK AND SAWYER

Milbank Mausoleum

York and Sawyer designed the Federal Reserve Bank of New York, the New York Historical Society, the New York Athletic Club and the Brick Presbyterian Church of New York.

About the Author

Edward F. Bergman is chairman of the Department of Geology and Geography at Herbert H. Lehman College (CUNY) in the Bronx. He received his undergraduate education at the University of Wisconsin and his Ph.D. in geography from the University of Washington. He did additional work at the University of Vienna, Austria.

He is the author of several books and numerous papers published in scholarly journals in the United States and abroad on New York City economics and urban planning, and on international economics. He is editorial correspondent in New York City for Parametro, one of Italy's leading periodicals of architecture and urban planning. He has been a visiting professor lecturing on New York City history and economy as well as supervisor for graduate theses on the subject of American urban studies at the University of Dublin, the University of Glasgow, the London School of Economics, the University of Brussels, the University of Amsterdam, the Technical University of Munich, the University of Frankfurt, the University of Bologna, the University of Rome and, occasionally, others.

Professor Bergman has taught both undergraduate and graduate college courses on American history and geography, New York local history and geography, international affairs and the history of economic ideas. He has chaired the development committee for a new course now required of all freshmen at Lehman College: "The Origins of the Modern World." This course work was funded by the National Endowment for the Humanities, and has received nationwide attention.

Photograph Credits

All photographs of The Woodlawn Cemetery were taken by Dominick Totino, and they are the property of The Woodlawn Cemetery.